Push
Play

Push Play

GAMING
FOR A
BETTER
WORLD

Songyee Yoon

Forbes | Books

Published by Forbes Books, Charleston, South Carolina.
An imprint of Advantage Media Group.

Forbes Books is a registered trademark, and the Forbes Books colophon is a trademark of Forbes Media, LLC.

Printed in the United States of America.

10 9 8 7 6 5 4 3 2 1

ISBN: 979-8-88750-082-9 (Hardcover)
ISBN: 979-8-88750-083-6 (eBook)

Library of Congress Control Number: 2023919724

Cover and layout design by Matthew Morse.

Since 1917, Forbes has remained steadfast in its mission to serve as the defining voice of entrepreneurial capitalism. Forbes Books, launched in 2016 through a partnership with Advantage Media, furthers that aim by helping business and thought leaders bring their stories, passion, and knowledge to the forefront in custom books. Opinions expressed by Forbes Books authors are their own. To be considered for publication, please visit **books.Forbes.com**.

*This book is dedicated to Ben and Daniel, who inspire me
and bring happiness to my life. I hope that you will have a world
full of opportunities where you can pursue your dreams without limits.*

CONTENTS

ACKNOWLEDGMENTS

During the process of creating this book, there were both challenging and enjoyable moments. I want to thank my colleagues who stood by me throughout the journey. With their support, we overcame obstacles and turned struggles into opportunities. I want to give a special shout-out to Ron for his unwavering dedication and patience during the tough times. He reminded us that persistence leads to success.

I also want to acknowledge MJ for their inspiring resilience and willingness to take on new challenges. To all my colleagues who offered their expertise, insights, and encouragement, thank you. We worked together and brought this book to life. Let the pages ahead reflect the spirit of collaboration and strength we found in one another.

Why Video Games?

The human predilection to play dates back all the way to our earliest recorded history. The Royal Game of Ur, a board game that dates back to 2600 BCE, was first discovered by Sir Leonard Woolley in a tomb at Ur in 1928. Several other copies have been found in other graves and tombs across the ancient world, even including King Tut's tomb.[1] Mancala, a rudimentary game including pebbles and indentations, also has an ancient past possibly dating back to Neolithic settlements from around 5600 BCE.[2] Even toys that can be played with alone or with friends have a deep history. Archaeologists have excavated ancient dolls with movable limbs that are akin to Barbie dolls on toy shelves across America today. We've always wanted to play. It's as natural to us as breathing.

When we play, we learn about ourselves and the world around us. As children, we rush to climb the highest tree to beat out our peers.

---

1   Deb Amlen, "The Royal Game of Ur: How to Play the Oldest Board Game on Record," New York Times, November 17, 2022, https://www.nytimes.com/2022/11/17/crosswords/ur-first-board-game.html.

2   Savannah African Art Museum, "Mancala," https://www.savannahafricanartmuseum.org/2020-workshops/05-2.

The first one to the top wins a stunning view of the neighborhood around them. Yet, as we play climb, we learn about how our body pulls itself through space. We develop fine motor skills, but that's just a secondary effect to the fun we're having with our friends. Because the play is the primary thing, we may not notice the skills and growth in ourselves. That secret to play is what makes it such an effective tool in the classroom and the workplace.

Play pushes us to take risks. When we're in competition during a game, we put everything on the line so we can feel that sense of victory. Think of soccer players in a tournament who desperately throw themselves toward the ball to score that last goal. But this drive is not only physical. It also shows up in the mental fortitude of a chess player who outthinks and outplays their opponent. When we play to win, we rethink what is possible and develop truly unique solutions. This mind-expanding nature of play makes it an invaluable tool for innovation and creativity.

Play connects us. By squaring off against our opponents, we learn about each other's strategies and perspectives. Maybe two opponents find common ground in a cooperative game. Or maybe they spar with each other to better develop their gameplay. Thanks to massively multiplayer online (MMO) gaming and other ways to play on the internet, humans are also able to play with people from other communities and cultures. This cross-cultural exchange in gaming allows us to consider our place in the world and how we relate to others in our communities. Whether it's playing at a local playground or with gamers from around the world, play brings us together to compete, to grow, and to change.

Today, video games represent our most modern approach to play. Whether it be through the latest console from Nintendo or Sony or on mobile games like *Candy Crush* on our phones, games compel us to think creatively, quickly, and collaboratively. The industry that conceptualizes, develops, creates, and markets these electronic experiences is a vital and growing part of the American economy. In 2022, traditional gaming and e-sports generated over $54.1 billion. By 2027, experts expect this to reach $72 billion,[3] and it's all because we love playing and the benefits we get from it. Video games allow us to have a richer human experience that expands our senses and our perceptions of the world.

> » Today, video games represent
> our most modern approach to play.

Yet video games and the gaming industry have been denounced and vilified since the first Ataris were flying off the shelves in the late '70s. Parents and other caretakers bemoan gaming as a waste of time that could be spent on other more worthwhile endeavors. Portrayals of gamers in the media show them as unmotivated and addicted individuals who are glued to their screens. Politicians even target video games as instigators of violence. Shortly after shootings in Texas in 2019, the then lieutenant governor Dan Patrick criticized the video game industry and claimed that it "teaches young people to kill."[4] Despite all the beneficial aspects of play, gaming is seen as a shameful and unproductive activity that's unsuited for growing children and completely unacceptable for grown adults.

---

3   Dean Takahashi, "Traditional Gaming Shrinks to 26.7% of Game and Esports Revenue as Overall US Sales Head to $72B by 2027," VentureBeat, June 2023.

4   Anthony Palumbi, *Video Games Don't Kill, Washington Post*, August 8, 2019, https://www.washingtonpost.com/opinions/2019/08/08/video-games-dont-kill-politicians-who-scapegoat-them-hit-real-anxiety/.

Gaming, however, has had a profound impact on me and my career. As an entrepreneur, I have seen how gaming has pushed forward innovations that would not have been possible in any other industry. I came into my role as president and chief strategy officer of NCSOFT, an MMO game development company, because I knew how gaming can connect us and teach us about each other. Knowing the impacts that gaming has on our development, I have stood up for educational programs that utilize techniques from gaming to unlock learning in students of all ages. Gaming is at the heart of all I do, and it baffles me that it has developed the reputation it has.

Which is why I am writing this book. I want to show you how gaming can be a force for good in the world. In the following chapters, you'll hear stories from my own life, research from experts, and real-world case studies that will demystify gaming and the video game industry. As humans, we need play to grow, to adapt, and to survive. The world of video games gives us that sandbox in which we can kick up the dirt and see what settles. Every day a new global issue arises. If we push play in everything we do, we open up new possibilities for humans and our collective existence on this planet.

CHAPTER ONE

Our Playful Instincts

How the instinct to play, programmed into our biology, teaches us valuable skills and motivates change in all species

For holiday, my family and I vacationed to the Galápagos Islands to immerse ourselves in nature. For a daylong excursion, we took to the beaches of this gorgeous archipelago to observe flora and fauna that we'd never find in the Bay Area. The island was unlike anything I had seen before—teeming with life that I'd only seen on *National Geographic* pages. After a guided hike through an island forest, we found ourselves on a cliff overlooking a small island surrounded by a small bay of crystal-clear water. Through the waves, we could see dozens of sea lions making their way to the beach of the secluded island.

On one side of this small island were about twenty smaller sea lions, which our guide identified for us as younger sea lion pups. We watched, from a distance, as the pups caught the surf, knocked each other off rocks, and chased each other around the island. Almost all day, they were a tangled and chaotic mess of youth. Amid all this energy sat one larger sea lion upon a rock in the shade, quietly observing their behavior. Our guide explained to us that these sea lion pups were playing while being watched over by the alpha male sea lion of the pod. Sea lions, they went on to say, have a long gestational period and only have, on average, one baby each year. For this reason, that one adult sea lion earnestly protects the young from any potential harm that might come to them.

Yet what we saw were sea lion pups getting quite aggressive with each other. Even from the cliffside, we could see the sea lions give each other bruises and scrapes. This rough play must have had some use if the guardian male sea lion was not intervening. I noticed that the ways these pups played on the beach were not dissimilar to what adult sea lions were doing on their hunts. When the pups surfed, they learned how to swim effectively. When they chased each other, they mimicked their hunt for prey. And when they pushed each other off a rock, they were practicing their territorial nature. Even though this play looked dangerous, the adult sea lion chaperone ensured no pup was injured, providing a risk-free space for them to practice being adults.

All animals play; it is an innate attribute of life on this planet. And the ways in which we play as humans are not dissimilar to the ways we observe animals playing. There are various reasons why animals play. As we see in the sea lion pups, animals will sometimes play to learn the skills they will need to deploy as adults. Outside of locomotive development, play develops an animal's social cues, allowing them to learn about themselves and the animals around them. Finally, play pushes boundaries, encouraging certain species to think differently and grow.

Despite all this, however, many human adults consider play to be a frivolous pastime that we should do away with. Gaming, as the natural evolution of play through technology, is often associated with laziness and a lack of productivity. The stereotypical gamer has been depicted as a sedentary person surrounded by flashing screens, contributing nothing to society. Anything excessive that interferes with a balanced lifestyle should be discouraged. However, a healthy dose of play does not need to be.

As the president and chief strategy officer of NCSOFT, an online gaming company, I have personally heard from many parents who fail to see the value in our games. As a parent myself, I try to limit screen time for my children. It can be difficult to limit play when more deference is given than can be handled. However, our innate drive to play continues to motivate us and keep us curious. The challenge should not completely eliminate the opportunity to grow through play. As a form of play, gaming has the power to help us learn skills, push our boundaries, and connect with each other.

HOW EVERYTHING PLAYS

Play is hardwired into our collective biology. Animals and humans come into the world with incompletely formed neuromuscular systems and behavior repertoires. To become competent adults, they must exercise and learn and practice behaviors essential to their survival later in life. Play is essential to survival. Younger animals play more than older ones because they have more to develop. For example, young coyotes play chase tag with each other to develop their hunting skills. Without play, adult animals would be poorly equipped for the tasks of life. They would not have developed the practical skills they need, nor would they have developed the social consciousness necessary to be competent members of their societies. In fact, there are serious developmental consequences when an animal is deprived of the play they need, which we will see later.

» Play is essential to survival.

So, before we get into how we play, how do we define it? Well, first off, as I observed with the sea lion pups on my Galápagos excursion, play is not exclusive to humans but can be found across species. While we can easily see it in our warm- or cold-blooded friends, like cats and dogs, even fish, frogs, and insects play.

Gordon Burghardt, professor of psychology and evolutionary biology at the University of Tennessee, Knoxville, sought to define this observed behavior in order to better understand it. In his research, he defines play as "a repeated and non-functional behavior that imitates adaptive behavior that the animal initiates when it is in a relaxed and low-stress setting."[5] But not all animals play the same. In fact, how an animal engages in this activity is programmed into their DNA.

As we know from our sea lion friends, play develops essential skills that individuals take into their adult lives. Human infants, for example, have two options for play, either with adults or with objects. Through these two spheres of play, they expand their senses, learning about their world and how it functions. Everything from object permanence to grasping their parents' fingers is fueled by the thousands and thousands of brain connections they're forging through play. In the first few months of our lives, our brains create more neural connections than they ever

---

5   Gordon Burghardt, "Play in Fishes, Frogs and Reptiles," *Current Biology* 25, no. 1 (January 5, 2015).

do again in our lives.[6] And how we play impacts the kind of adults we become and how we differ from our peers.

Different animals play differently. Hunting animals like lions and cougars stalk their prey as adults. In preparation, lion cubs stalk and pounce on each other to imitate adult hunting behavior to ensure they can catch that antelope when the time comes.[7] Prey animals, on the other hand, play in ways that help them to elude the advances of their pursuers. Deer, antelope, and their other hooved relatives play in a way that resembles the human game of tag: chasing each other in a group and then scattering from the one who is "it." This behavior builds the locomotive skills needed to avoid becoming the dinner for their predator.[8]

We can extend this to how humans, even as adults, play differently. As we grow, we develop our own interests like art, sports, or STEM (science, technology, engineering, and mathematics) that are related to how we played as children. My own interest in computers, as a matter of fact, came wrapped in a computer game called *Knightmare*, contained on one eight-inch floppy disc. My friends and I would push this game into our computers and be transported to a pixelated world replete with evil Hudnos. The more familiar we became with the game, however, the more we realized we could manipulate it to obtain more points or warp to future levels. Learning and practicing the ways to get these "Easter eggs" sparked my interest in coding and computer science. And my experience is not unique. Children who play at jumping and climbing may develop interests that allow them

---

6   Diana Bales, "The Importance of Play in Baby's Brain Development," University of Georgia, Extension, September 1, 2014.

7   Lalibela Game Reserve, "Lion Cubs Growing Up in the Wild," https://lalibela.net/lion-cubs-growing-up-in-the-wild-blog/.

8   John A. Byers, "Play in Ungulates," in Smith (1984), 43–65.

to flex their muscles. In contrast, young artists derive their skills from playing at drawing and imagining.

We also develop social skills from play that help us interact with others. One study shows that young apes play using their faces and hands to experiment with gestures that take on deeper meanings as they grow into adults. These gestures form the basis for their society, creating roles and connections that ensure the overall success of the tribe.[9] And this kind of behavior is not solely exhibited by mammals. Some species of spiders play in order to test the limits of their social order. For example, male spiders imitate mating with female spiders in order to become more effective lovers in their future endeavors. Indeed, the research shows that male spiders who repeatedly engaged in "mock mating" fathered more eggs than those that did not. This play, however, does not come without its own risks—a female who catches a male in the act devours him on the spot.[10] These examples show that playing has implications for how we see ourselves, and how we define our roles in society.

Humans play to learn their roles, too, although it's far less grizzly than the spider version. Observe young toddlers dressing up to pretend they're shop owners or teachers and see how they take on adult gestures and rules. In these imagined scenarios, they simulate how adults interact and test out social norms to see how they operate. Through this play, they learn about the adult world and grow a set of values and perspectives unique to their experience. Babies even learn to communicate nonverbally by mocking the facial expressions of the adults around them. These social skills developed through imagined play allow them to understand the world and how they fit into it.

---

9   Fröhlich, Wittig, and Pika, "Play-Solicitation Gestures in Chimpanzees in the Wild: Flexible Adjustment to Social Circumstances and Individual Matrices," *Royal Society Open Science* 3, no. 8 (August 2016).

10   Susan Milus, "Spider Sex Play Speeds Up Successful Mating," *Wired*, January 2011.

Animals who do not get the chance to play, however, may experience difficulty adapting to their surroundings. For example, captive creatures that live in barren environments, with no toys or enrichment activities, have higher levels of stress hormones that harm their immune system and hamper brain development. They may even take to hurting themselves. Ravens deprived of play may peck at their own feathers or beat their wings against cages.[11] Play deprivation in human children is no less damaging. Children who cannot play freely have a harder time connecting with their peers and have a higher propensity for anxiety and depression.[12] While the saying may be clichéd, an "all work and no play" mindset will have serious consequences on one's development.

Play gives us all the practice we need to take on the challenges of adulthood, but it does not come without its own challenges. This would not be a book about gaming if I did not mention that playing always comes with a risk of losing. Learning happens when we are allowed to play, risk, and fail in a safe environment. It's why the elder sea lion watched over the younger ones as they played chase on the beach. And it's no different for us humans. It's why we're drawn to exciting adventures, like skydiving, roller coasters and video games. Play expands our concept of what is possible.

> » Play expands our concept
> of what is possible.

By putting ourselves into playful situations where we can fail, we test out new skills that may seem difficult or impossible at first. With continued practice, however, we overcome that feeling and

---

11   Alan Yu, "Which Animals Play and Why?" (podcast), *The Pulse*, WHYY, August 2019.

12   Richard Hywood, "The Impact of Play Deprivation," *TSW*, August 2022.

unlock new possibilities that prepare us for more difficult challenges later in life. Just like when you beat that hard boss you couldn't get past in your last video game and the game makes you drop the armor that prepared you for the rest of the game. Play also helps us think up new solutions to existing problems. You can credit play and gaming with many advances in the tech space. Playing helps us innovate new solutions and work together on teams. Play gives us the tools to move forward.

PLAY CREATES THE IMPOSSIBLE

When I was growing up in South Korea, my father always encouraged me to make my own decisions. In Korea, parents often prefer boys over girls for reasons deeply entrenched in the culture. Due to this, raising my sister and me could have been a disappointment to my father, but he never let that show. Despite the societal pressure, he embraced having a family of women. That being said, he never treated us like typical "girls." He'd go away on business trips and return with his suitcase full of toys for the two of us. But he didn't bring home Barbies.

Dancing robots, automatic racing cars, and gizmos with flashing lights spilled out of his suitcase onto our bedroom floor. While I loved to play with these toys, I was more curious about what on the inside made them tick.

So, while my dad was at work, I'd spend whole afternoons dismantling his gifts to see what made the lights blink, the robots dance, and the cars go so fast. I was fascinated by the circuits, the switches, and the boards that made these friends of mine spring to life. Before he'd get home, I'd expertly put them all back together so that no one was the wiser. I mention my childhood because, at that time in South Korea, a young girl interested in technology was a fable.

14

Girls had a very specific path. Their destiny was to get married and start a family to feed and care for. However, I knew this couldn't be the extent of my life. Dismantling and repairing the toys from my father cultivated in me a curiosity for technology that I couldn't ignore.

My father always supported me in pursuing my interests even if they went against what society expected from me. Starting when I was young, he made sure I had a safe space to express my desires and find my place in the world. One year during Chuseok, a three-day autumn festival in Korea, my father made this commitment public. You see, Chuseok is a Korean festival that draws an imaginary line down Korean households that separates men from women. Mothers, grandmothers, and sisters would spend this holiday in the kitchen, delicately folding, steaming, and frying mandu, Korean dumplings filled with pork, beef, and cabbage. Meanwhile, fathers, grandfathers, and brothers would sit at the table, chowing down on mandu and drinking baeksaeju. The women would serve the perfectly shaped mandu to the men before retreating back to the kitchen to eat the broken and misshapen dumplings.

I used to dread when mandu time came around. My little fingers, so adept at taking apart machinery, were no match for the dumpling wrappers that were plopped in front of me. I watched in frustration while other women wrapped perfect coin-purse-size dumplings with the exact number of folds. I struggled the most during dinnertime at Chuseok. The uncles and male cousins were seated together at a large table in the living room, where perfectly shaped and cooked mandu were served. Meanwhile, my aunts and female cousins and I were relegated to the kitchen, where ugly or popped dumplings were offered. As Chuseok was a holiday for the entire family, I found it difficult to understand why we had to be separated in this way.

So, I marched into the living room and politely asked my father if I could sit at the table with him instead. Without hesitation, he made a space next to him where I could sit and enjoy my pretty dumplings for the rest of the night. That evening, I learned to ask for my seat at the table. After that, my father always made sure I followed my curiosity. Many times, I found myself the only girl participating in math or science competitions, but he was always there to support me. He cheered me on, provided me with transportation, and gave me the courage to keep going. Through it all, my dad made sure that I could take risks and play at my own pace to grow as a person.

I first joined NCSOFT, the leading game development company behind titles such as *Lineage* and *Guild Wars*, because we shared a mission—to push play. More than just hitting a button on a console, we push the boundaries on what play can be and how it shapes mankind. We use play to create worlds where everyone can see themselves and grow. For the past fifteen years, I have led our company through multiple game launches, new monetization strategies, and an innovative artificial intelligence transformation that stands to revolutionize the way we design games. It's been my great pleasure to see our initially small team grow to include thousands from across seven countries in Asia, North America, and Europe. Our mission remains the same as when I first joined: to press what play can do for us and to make people happier by connecting them.

That's precisely why I wish to delve into the topic of play with you through this book. It's truly remarkable that the concept of play, which is so fundamental to our humanity, remains misunderstood by so many. Every day should have some element of play. As we have seen, play has the power to teach us invaluable skills. Even as adults, there is research that proves how simulated play increases efficiency. Play also helps us learn about ourselves and the society we live in. At NCSOFT, we work to create gaming worlds where people can connect, work together, and reimagine what our reality can be. And finally, play pushes us to innovate. In fact, the gaming industry's playful nature has been the source of many innovations that the tech industry uses today. Business models such as microtransactions and subscriptions, for example, all have their roots in the gaming community. There is so much we can learn from play, and I hope to share just a small part of that with you.

Next time you see an animal playing, whether it be your dog chasing a fetch or your cat batting around their toy, think about the ways you can bring a playful nature to your day. Perhaps there's a skill or hobby you keep putting down because you can't find the time to practice or because the failure frustrates you. How can you reimagine that practice time as play time?

While our brains become more rigid as we age, play still provides a mental flexibility that gives us the chance to try something new. Even educators see how gaming and play can be used to both teach children and train adults on the job.

Our brains crave this exercise, and in the next chapter, we'll dive deep into how we learn through play and how you can use playful skills to power up your own nerdiness.

CHAPTER TWO

Gaming Changes Us

When we game, our brain is activated in a different way—one that has the potential to open up new perspectives and combat implicit bias.

South Korea is one of the most connected countries in the world. Starting as early as the midnineties, the internet has been widely used in Korean education and research. In 2004, as broadband connections were becoming available to average citizens, over eleven million Koreans had broadband connected in their homes—over 70 percent of the country's population.[13] In the same year in the United States, only 19.1 percent of households were wired to the internet through broadband.[14] Today, South Korea continues to outpace the United States in terms of connected households and internet speed. According to a recent study, 99.2 percent of South Korean households

---

13 K. Chon et al., "A Brief History of the Internet in Korea," August 29, 2005, http://www.columbia.edu/~hauben/netizens/tunis-ppf/KChon.doc.

14 US Department of Commerce, National Telecommunications and Information Administration, *A Nation Online: Entering the Broadband Age*, September 2004.

now have broadband access, compared to the US at only 85 percent.[15] Thanks to this massive infrastructure, connectivity is a deep part of our culture.

Despite these connections, however, there is a huge divide between the educational systems in rural and urban communities in South Korea. Classrooms in major urban centers such as Seoul are better equipped to serve their students than those in the rural areas. This puts those students that live in rural areas at an incredible disadvantage. With a lack of quality education, these students are unable to attain well-paying jobs, which, in turn, means they are unable to build wealth or influence. With low wages, these communities stay impoverished, and the gap between these two communities continues to grow, creating more inequity. In a country where connectivity is a symbol of national pride, it is disheartening to see this clear break between the two parts of our society.

Hodoo English, an immersive role-playing game that teaches English, was developed to address this issue exactly. Codeveloped by NCSOFT, the MMORPG allows players to collect "chunks" of English phrases by observing interactions in a world of over three hundred non-player characters. Players then use these phrases in other scenarios to gain points that they can trade in to update their avatar's appearance or to purchase furniture and decorations for their in-game home. Players demonstrate their knowledge in "Chunk Hunting Battles" where they must correctly identify the phrase by listening, speaking the phrase into their microphone, reading the phrase, and writing the phrase out. For accurately doing all four, players also gain points and the ability to use the phrase in other scenarios.

---

15   E. Ramirez, "Nearly 100% of Households in South Korea Now Have Internet Access, Thanks to Seniors," *Forbes*, January 31, 2017, https://www.forbes.com/sites/ elaineramirez/2017/01/31/nearly-100-of-households-in-south-korea-now-have- internet-access-thanks-to-seniors.

Through the power of South Korea's broadband connection, *Hodoo English* was available for everyone who had access to the internet. Students from across South Korea used *Hodoo English* to teach themselves English. Many of these players may never have access to an English class, which is often unaffordable to kids from underprivileged backgrounds. But through our open-world gameplay, they immerse themselves in the language, one of the most effective ways to learn a new language. What's more, they are able to connect with other players who are learning English to practice their language skills. *Hodoo English* doesn't just teach a new language. It opens up new opportunities for the future of its players.

Gaming can change us. Through games like *Hodoo English*, we can provide meaningful learning experiences that have the potential to change us for the better. And the learning and growth from gaming isn't just about acquiring new skills. Recent research shows that gaming changes our brain's structure. In emerging gaming technology, there may even be therapeutic applications to help those who need it. And gaming has the potential to democratize learning, opening up new opportunities for communities of people that may not have access to those resources.

> » **Gaming changes our brain's structure.**

OUR BRAINS ON GAMING

When the Atari 2600 became commercially available and video games began to dominate the public narrative, there was a prevailing notion that gaming would rot your brain. In the United States, parents and politicians both had deep concerns about the effects that games had

21

on their children. In the late '90s and early 2000s, US senators and congresspeople from every spectrum of the political system held summits, press conferences, and meetings about the violent effect of video games on our youths and the aggressive tendencies they may or may not cause. Even today, there is a generally negative view of the online gamer with a comically large gaming setup with a snack-stained keyboard and a tricked-out desk and chair. Through all of these, there's a stereotype that gaming can only negatively affect your body.

What's so silly about this argument is that it simply isn't true. In 2014, a collaborative effort across institutions explored the cognitive landscapes of adolescents who were deeply engaged in video game play, spending up to twelve hours per week immersed in digital environments. This group invited scrutiny that went beyond conventional neuroscientific inquiry. The study included a diverse group of gamers, covering both male and female players. Advanced neuroimaging technologies were used to identify the cerebral signatures of this group and compare them to those who did not play video games, shedding light on profound cognitive differences.

A narrative of anatomical divergence emerged from this study, particularly in the areas of visual acuity and motor coordination. Interestingly, those who were deeply engaged in video games exhibited a heightened state of maturation in these areas, indicative of cognitive prowess. This trajectory culminated in a cerebral nexus marked by augmented cortical connectivity, specifically toward the left dorsolateral prefrontal cortex (DLPFC), the bastion of executive function and judgment.[16] This cerebral locus exhibited heightened cortical coherence, suggesting a correlation between gaming engagement and cognitive governance.

---

16   S. Kühn et al, IMAGEN Consortium, "Positive Association of Video Game Playing
      with Left Frontal Cortical Thickness in Adolescents," *PLoS One*, March 14, 2014.

The findings of this study had far-reaching implications. The increased cortical thickness found in this group was associated with augmented manual dexterity, the interplay between hand and ocular prowess, and the finesse exhibited in tracing the trajectories of spatial entities. This monumental study illustrated a story of neurocognitive metamorphosis—a testament to the transformative potential of video game engagement upon our brains.

In fact, there have been various other studies that show that video gaming impacts how we see. Another prevailing notion about video games is that those who play them may have a shorter attention span. This, however, was not the case when researchers tested the attention of those who play action video games. To ascertain gamers' ability to pay attention, the researchers administered an Attentional Network Test (ANT), which challenges participants to keep track of certain cues and avoid others. The ANT also provides off-task activities that the player must ignore. When the researchers compared the ANT scores of gamers to nongamers, they found that gamers had enhanced attention skills that allowed them to make faster and more accurate decisions. Gamers were able to track multiple objects moving at a faster speed than their nongamer friends. They were also able to filter out more unimportant information, better understand how a three-dimensional object exists in space, and switch more easily from tasks than their counterparts.[17]

As gaming technology has evolved and educators have taken note of its power in molding the mind, there have been many attempts to bring these innovations into the classroom. One of the most popular of these is virtual reality technology, or VR. It may surprise you to learn that the first deployment of VR technology in the classroom was

---

[17] M. W. Dye, C. S. Green, and D. Bavelier, "The Development of Attention Skills in Action Video Game Players, *Neuropsychologia*, July 2009.

all the way back in 1966. Thomas Furness, an engineer for the US Air Force, built a VR display that mounted inside a pilot's helmet to use as a flight simulator for pilots waiting on their planes to be serviced. As VR technology became more available through the next half a century, there have been various instances where VR benefitted students through immersive experiences and gamification techniques.[18] Despite its success in individual cases, VR has failed to gain widespread acceptance in the classroom. This may be due to the technology itself.

While the tech industry made big bets on the metaverse and virtual reality in early 2023, there are real issues with VR technology that should have given them pause. With the Oculus Rift, VR has become more commercially available for the everyday consumer. Oliver Roeder, a journalist with the *Financial Times*, detailed his "surprising [and] scary experience of the metaverse" in a review of the technology.[19] He notes that many, including himself, experience nausea while in the headset. Described as "stomach awareness," some users feel a vertigo-inducing drop when flying through these virtual worlds. Additionally, using the wands that come with the headset sometimes can present a hazard to furniture or others not present in the virtual world. Finally, the current graphical display contains many flaws that seem amusing, including, in Roeder's words, putting on a baseball cap that was comically too large for his avatar's head.

While VR has struggled to gain its footing and the metaverse seems like a risky bet, this technology may be able to help those struggling through dark times. For patients with posttraumatic stress disorder (PTSD), exposure therapy, where a patient is exposed to a

---

18   S. Kavanagh, A. Luxton-Reilly, B. Wuensche, and B. Plimmer. "A Systematic Review of Virtual Reality in Education," *Themes in Science and Technology Education* 10, no. 2 (2017), http://earthlab.uoi.gr/theste.

19   Oliver Roeder, "On Your Marks, Headset, Go: My Surprising, Scary Trip to the Metaverse, Financial Times, February 24, 2023, https://www.ft.com/content/151b1d9b-4eb3-4016-a20e-75c387b94e0b.

stimulus that triggers negative symptoms, is an effective treatment. Yet, successfully delivering this therapy to patients is very difficult. Many patients who undergo this therapy drop out of the treatment— with some researchers citing shockingly low completion rates.[20]

With virtual reality exposure therapy (VRET), however, therapists use VR technology to deliver these stimuli to their patients in a controlled setting. Therapists are also able to scale the impact of the stimuli to their patient's comfort level. While still in initial trials, VRET has promising results for those with PTSD, social anxiety, social phobias, and other triggering conditions.[21]

While we explored how play impacts our development as young children in previous chapters, these recent studies have shown that play through gaming can leave lasting impressions—even on adults. Gamers see the world differently, perhaps thanks to more developed parts of the brain. They're able to track objects more effectively in space, allowing them to make faster decisions and to better understand a shape's dimensions in space. Finally, gaming has pushed forward VR technology, a potentially useful tool in the classroom and in therapeutic settings. From my perspective, none of these examples seem detrimental to our brains, and in fact, some represent a cerebral enhancement. Yet some people still claim video games have a negative impact simply by existing. Gaming itself is not inherently bad. Negative biases around gaming, however, continue to blind society to the positive impacts of gaming. Biases are hard to break. The key to breaking them may also lie in gaming.

20   Z. Imel et al., "Meta-Analysis of Dropout in Treatments for Posttraumatic Stress Disorder," *Journal of Consulting and Clinical Psychology* 81, no. 3 (January 31, 2013).

21   R. Gonçalves et al., "Efficacy of Virtual Reality Exposure Therapy in the Treatment of PTSD: A Systematic Review, *PLoS One*, 2012.

MIND-EXPANDING PLAY

Early in my career, I worked as a consultant at McKinsey, a management consulting firm, helping clients better understand their problems and how to solve them. My time at McKinsey taught me how to think differently and analyze fast. Despite this, there were other learning curves that came with the job I didn't expect. One of my main responsibilities during this time was to lead focus group sessions, and workshops with my clients. Many of my clients were tech companies dominated by the chief executives, all men, who towered over the rest of the board. In many client engagements, these male leaders would hire McKinsey, expecting a foreign (American) male consultant that would help them through their issues. When I showed up to the first meeting, they often confused me with a translator, there to assist their consultant. They just didn't expect a consultant could also be a woman. Their bias colored their perspective of me.

In one instance, one of my clients was so shocked by my gender they almost lost McKinsey's service. The room was set up for a workshop, and the clients were all seated ready to get started. I took the podium and had begun my presentation when one client stopped me to ask when the consultant was arriving. When I informed him that I was the team lead for this McKinsey study, he refused. He said he could not work with a team led by a woman. So, I did the only thing I could do—I waited while McKinsey made their choice. Instead of getting rid of me, however, the leaders at McKinsey removed other teams from the client's organization, citing cultural differences. When the client saw that, he politely agreed to work with my team and me and bashfully requested the other teams back as well.

While we've seen how play can build skills, we also play to imagine new realities. I tell you this story to demonstrate how a lack of imagination can empower a person's bias, which in turn can have insidious implications. The executive from my story, I assume, had only ever interacted with other men in his position. From his experience, he created an idea of what a consultant "should" look like. He could not imagine a consultant that looked like me. That bias shaped the way he interacted with me and the larger McKinsey organization. And his lack of imagination almost cost him hundreds of thousands of dollars.

To understand how bias can impact our worldview, take a look at the toy aisle of your local big box store. While much has changed in recent years, I expect there are toys that one would consider stereotypically "masculine" and "feminine." These definitions, however, reflect how our society views gender and, in turn, reinforces those stereotypes. In one study, researchers found that toys marketed toward boys were typically "violent, competitive, exciting and somewhat dangerous." Those toys meant for girls, however, were nurturing and associated with domestic skills or physical appearance.[22] What's more, even something like "creativity" has been coded as feminine by implicit bias. Based on responses from over seven thousand parents, another study showed that parents encouraged their daughters to engage in play activities that are performative, creative, and dramatic, and their sons with things that are related to exploration, curiosity, and STEM.[23] These studies show how these biases exist right where our perspectives are first taking form—in our sense of play.

The way we play as children impacts how we lead our adult lives. These gendered stereotypes begin taking hold as early as age six! When girls are told that engineering and STEM are "boy subjects," they believe it and begin to enforce those stereotypes among their

---

22   J. E. O. Blakemore and R. E. Centers, "Characteristics of Boys' and Girls' Toys," *Sex Roles* 53 (November 2005), https://doi.org/10.1007/s11199-005-7729-0.

23   The Geena Davis Institute on Gender in Media, "LEGO Group Creativity Study," 2021.

play groups.[24] As they grow up and turn into gamers, that bias affects their game choice with many girls avoiding strategy- and STEM-based games due to insecurity around how good they will be at those games.[25] This false narrative extends through their educational careers, where girls avoid science and engineering classes that they've been told are not for them. And as they graduate, these women are less likely to pursue careers in STEM because they have just not been exposed to it.

This vicious cycle of bias deprives many organizations of great workers, and we all must consider how we can break the cycle. One way may be in how we talk about science in the classroom. As mentioned previously, children begin to assign certain aspects to gender from an early age. They are more likely to say, for example, that a woman is "a mommy" and a man is "a scientist." But how do they feel about girls "doing science"? A study from New York University showed that girls were more engaged with STEM topics when an instructor used action verbs instead of identifiers when discussing science. To test this, researchers presented a group of girls aged four to nine with the opportunity to play a game that was about the scientific method. They found that the girls who were told they were "doing science" stayed engaged with the game longer than those who were told by the instructor to "be scientists."[26] A girl's interest impacts how she sees herself in the world—it shapes her identity. Encouraging them to be active participants in science, however, may help them see themselves in a STEM field.

---

24 A. Master, A. Meltzoff, and S. Cheryan, "Gender Stereotypes about Interests Start Early and Cause Gender Disparities in Computer Science and Engineering, *PNAS* 118, no. 48 (November 22, 2021).

25 M. Flanagan and G. Kaufman, "Shifting Implicit Biases with Games Using Psychology," in *Diversifying Barbie and Mortal Kombat: Intersectional Perspectives and Inclusive Designs in Gaming*, March 2017.

26 S. Sparks, "To Encourage Girls in Science, Talk Action, Not Identity, *EdWeek*, February 7, 2019, https://www.edweek.org/teaching-learning/to-encourage-girls-in-science-talk-action-not-identity/2019/02.

Another reason why girls feel less confident to identify as scientists may be due to the lack of women in STEM roles. We know that representation is one of the best ways to combat implicit bias.[27] By promoting women and other underrepresented groups into leadership roles, our mental image of who can fill these roles changes. The lack of female representation in the STEM field overall may discourage young girls from pursuing their curiosity for science, math, and technology. Again, we see that the problem is structural and self-fulfilling. To combat bias and create an equitable world, women must be represented in every field at every level. A big shake-up is needed—one that will be felt in all areas of society.

For my part, it is my personal mission to usher in this sea change and create more opportunities for women in business. At NCSOFT, we have more women in our C-suite than any other tech company in South Korea. But that's not where our commitment ends: women are represented in almost every role in our company to ensure that our products are created with their valuable perspective. Outside of NCSOFT, I continue this work in my partnership with several nonprofit groups across the world. One of these is the Asia Pacific Foundation of Canada (APF Canada), the leading organization for research, analysis, and consultation on Canada-Asia relations. Through APF Canada, I cochair women-only business missions where female entrepreneurs and leaders from business, tech, and government meet to discuss the unique challenges they face and to network with their peers. These talented, dynamic groups of female entrepreneurs are inspiring examples of how women can support and uplift each other.

---

27 J. L. Shropshire and K. L. Johnson, "Harnessing Visible Representation to Mitigate Bias," *Policy Insights from the Behavioral and Brain Sciences* 8, no 1 (February 11, 2021), https://doi.org/10.1177/2372732220984800.

Radical action is needed to make our world a better place for everyone, and these cohorts of women leaders are only one part of that shake up. Thanks to innovations in technology, we are able to make connections with people from across the world. Our communities are becoming more global every day. As our world grows smaller, we must also consider what kind of world we want to create, and who we will leave it to. What will the young girl who wants to be a scientist do if the opportunity is not provided to her as equally as it is to her male peer? Our work begins by opening up opportunities for everyone, regardless of age, gender, religion, nationality, or location.

> » **Radical action is needed to make our world a better place for everyone.**

When we first launched *Hodoo English*, it was imperative that the software was available to anyone who wanted to learn English. By taking cues from massively multiplayer online role-playing game (MMORPG) design, we created a community of learners who could support each other in their educational journeys. When we play, we stretch our imaginations to dream up new worlds where anything is possible. Play has the power to free us from this bias and gaming can be a powerful tool that can expand someone's perspective. Finally, gaming can be used to change the way we see the world, allowing for a space to wonder and create. These three qualities—accessibility, community, and wonder—are essential tools to creating a more equitable world. When we're all invited to play in the way that feels authentic to us, we expand our perspectives, share valuable ideas, support each other, and have the potential to change the world.

CHAPTER THREE

Playing for Discovery

> Gaming enhances our sense of wonder and discovery. Here's how scientists and business people can harness that sense of curiosity to innovate and solve the world's biggest problems.

What is possible if we let a child follow their curiosity? This was the driving question that led to the foundation of the Projectory, a third space between home and school for Korean students to explore their curiosity and passions. In this space, the NC Cultural Foundation, a nonprofit organization sponsored by NCSOFT, aims to create an environment, a community, a paradigm that provides youths with more room for creative experiments and open explorations. The Projectory brings together students from all across Korea, including rural underserved areas, and gives them the tools and materials to build whatever they want. Replete with cardboard, wires, construction paper, and pipe cleaners, the Projectory provides the students with a lab to research, prototype, and test their creations. Within this membership-based community, Projectory members actively lead and engage their own projects without outside judgments and restrictions.

In addition to providing these materials, supervisors help guide the students in their pursuits but do not provide "instructional guidance." We do this to break away from the traditional model of education that is heavily focused on effective delivery of knowledge, the status quo for classrooms in South Korea and the United States. This stereotypical pedagogy uplifts the teacher as the holder of knowledge who dispenses it to their students. This pedagogy, however, is antithetical to the Projectory's mission. We encourage a flat hierarchy at the Projectory in two ways. First, we eliminate honorifics that are commonly used by Korean students when speaking with their teachers. And second, the supervisors at the Projectory are only there to assist the students in their projects—they do not teach. By allowing the students of the Projectory to wonder, tinker, and experiment, we strengthen the skills that they will use when they solve the problems of tomorrow.

After watching a handcycle race on television, a Projectory participant became fascinated with the operation of the simple machine. Under the supervision of Projectory staff, he researched the mechanics to better understand how the vehicle fit together. He then mapped out a design for his own handcycle—one that would fit his smaller frame. With materials provided by the Projectory, he built out the disparate parts and then put them together. There was only one thing left—to see if it worked. When asked how he would test it, he responded: "I'm going to ride it home." But he lived over forty miles away! It would take a half hour in a car to get there. But, the team at the Projectory didn't want to stand in the way of a beta test. Twenty minutes later, the student called his mom to pick him up. "It works," he said. "I learned that I should have built in a brake. But I believe it was still a success. I learned an important lesson."

At the Projectory, we create an environment where students can dream up anything and present them with the challenge of making that dream a reality. In this self-motivated learning, students learn about engineering, math, and computer science through the challenges they set for themselves. Their sense of accomplishment after they complete a project solidifies what they learned, giving them ownership over their progress. If they fail, they analyze why with our supervisors so that they learn from their mistakes. Once they've completed one project, they move on to the next—full of new insights, failures, and successes that continue to push their curiosity. In this way, we make learning more like playing at the Projectory.

Gaming also challenges us to learn. Gaming primes our curiosity. Games present us with difficult situations like puzzles, enemies, and quests. By accomplishing these challenges, the player is rewarded in various ways. This can be progressing through the story or receiving a valuable item or piece of equipment; or, as is the case in some puzzle games, completing the task is an achievement in itself. Good game designers know that balancing the challenge with the reward is key. If the reward feels paltry to the challenge set, gamers will become frustrated and give up. Should the challenge be easy and the reward great, however, a player may blaze through the game or grow bored with it. And each person's idea of a reward is different! A game where you collect bells to buy furnishings for your island village, for example, has its own reward structure while another game may challenge you to travel to distant lands to conquer various foes to save a princess. In each of these, however, we learn things about the world of the game through these challenges.

There is a link between gaming and curiosity. Playing a game makes us wonder and gives us new perspectives on problems. In cooperative play, we work together over problems presented to us, allowing us to harness the intellect and perspective of many over just one. Many scientists have seen the value in this collective problem-solving and have employed game design theories into their research. Our curiosity is what makes us human. It's our superpower. And through games, we can maximize its potential to gain new insights, advancing research forward for the benefit of us all.

> » **There is a link between gaming and curiosity.**

DISCOVERY THROUGH GAMING

As scientific research has progressed in this early part of our century, the questions that researchers have been tasked to answer have become increasingly large. Due to advances in technology, science is tackling bigger and more complex problems than ever before. And they're moving fast. As of 2018, more scientists are getting into their labs, and more funding for research has become available than ever before.[28] This has resulted in a huge push for discovery and innovation in various industries. Problems like addressing climate change or curing devastating diseases are on the docket for these scientists who wish to change the world through their research. Despite all this, however, researchers have come upon complicated problems that require thousands and thousands of hours of labor. While there are more

---

28   P. Collison and M. Nielsen, "Science Is Getting Less Bang for Its Buck," *The Atlantic*, November 16, 2018.

scientists than ever before, the work of discovery is too much for even these experts.[29]

In order to tackle these complex problems, some scientists have taken to crowdsourcing their research in a new field of study known as citizen science. First coined by ornithologist Rick Bonney, citizen science is the democratic public participation in scientific research that encourages everyday people to learn more about scientific research.[30] Bonney first used concepts related to this method of research in his ornithology study known as Project FeederWatch. In Project FeederWatch, enthusiastic birdwatchers sign up to count the number and types of birds they find eating seeds out of their feeders or in their backyards. Established ornithologists then use this data for various applications—from tracking winter migrations to better understanding how climate change impacts a bird's population.[31] Since then, this powerful new style of research has exploded into thousands of research projects that harness the curiosity of everyday people.

As mentioned previously, games have the potential to prime our curiosity. Knowing this, many researchers have begun to create citizen science games that assist them in their research. One example of this gamified research process is *EyeWire*, a game where players map the neurons of the human eye. Neurons are incredibly small, and we have an immense number of them—almost eighty billion in the human brain alone.[32] Knowing how these billions of miniscule branches make connections to each other is vital in understanding how our eye works. It can also help in the research for curing many neurodegenerative

---

29   Collison and Nielsen, "Science."

30   B. Strasser et al., "Citizen Science? Rethinking Science and Public Participation," Science and Technology Studies 32, no. 2 (May 5, 2019).

31   Project FeederWatch Overview, https://feederwatch.org/about/project-overview/.

32   *EyeWire: A Game to Crowdsource Brain Mapping*, https://www.citizenscience.gov/assets/files/eyewire-brain-mapping.pdf.

diseases. Thanks to new technology, scientists are able to map these neurons and their connections, but it is incredibly time consuming for one neuroscientist to do so. To map just a single section of these neurons can take up to ten hours. Mapping these neurons, however, doesn't require a doctorate or any other advanced degree. All you need is a love for solving puzzles.

EyeWire turns what could be a tedious process for one scientist into a game for everyone. When a user logs into their *EyeWire* account for the first time, they go through a tutorial that shows them how to map the neurons—a fairly simple point and click on the cross section of a retina sample that slowly becomes a three-dimensional model of the mapped neuron. As players map more neurons, they gain points that place them on a leaderboard for bragging rights to their peers. In some instances, certain players spent over fifty hours a week playing the game, building the connections between the neurons that help us see. Underscored by peppy and brain-empowering electronic beats, *EyeWire* really feels like a game, but it's important neurological wirings they discover—not armor or lore. Equipped with the knowledge of over two hundred thousand players from 150 countries, these scientists increase their computational power tenfold. *EyeWire* allows these experts to focus on the implications of this data rather than spending endless hours tracking it down themselves.[33]

The learning that happens in games is also progressive. Meaning, with each challenge you accomplish, the next challenge will be more difficult. For a citizen science game, however, the challenges not only become more difficult but also become more realistic, and solving the puzzle becomes more valuable to the research. Developed by scientists in collaboration with Stanford Medicine, *EteRNA* challenges

---

33   *EyeWire: A Game to Crowdsource Brain Mapping,* https://www.citizenscience.gov/ assets/files/eyewire-brain-mapping.pdf.

players to create links in RNA strands to better understand genetic engineering technology. Within the first few levels, *EteRNA* presents the player with puzzles where the patterns can be discerned quite easily, and you get to a solution quickly. But as the game progresses, the links become less clear, making it more difficult to solve. In turn, the solutions provided by the game's players become more useful to the research team, allowing them to gain deeper insights into how we can change and mold RNA.[34]

Some citizen science games have even figured out how to incorporate cooperative play into their gamified research. Scientists and game designers at the University of Washington created *FoldIt*, a game that challenges players to work individually or in teams to deduce the structure of individual proteins. These molecules are among the most basic structures needed for life. For all living things to operate, protein structures must fold and link together to trigger various functions throughout the organism. *FoldIt* leverages a gamer's advanced three-dimensional problem-solving skills to better understand these building blocks of life and how they can be used in medical research. When playing in a team, players compete to find the most natural structure for the protein, compete for points, and collaborate with other players and scientists through a chat system not unlike the one we use for *Lineage*.[35]

As one of the most established and most successful citizen science games, *FoldIt* has provided scientists with valuable insights that have unlocked breakthroughs for their research team. One of the biggest discoveries was the solution to a protein related to an AIDS-like virus that could prove groundbreaking for future medical research. What's even more impressive is that the work from these game players is

---

34   J. Lee et al., "RNA Design Rules from a Massive Open Laboratory," *Proceedings of the National Academy of Sciences* 111, no. 6 (February 11, 2014).

35   V. Curtis, "Online Citizen Science Games: Opportunities for the Biological Sciences," *Applied & Translational Genomics*, July 4, 2014.

outperforming the software that previously analyzed protein structures. *FoldIt* players' efforts have vastly improved the algorithm used to understand these proteins—even going so far as to rework a protein structure that was initially designed by a computer.[36] For amateurs with no real training in biochemistry, this is a remarkable discovery, and one that was made possible only through the power of gaming.

PLAYING FOR INNOVATION

Games aren't just distractions that entertain us—they are also a tool for discovery. By placing challenges in front of us, games exercise our problem-solving skills, and by engaging in games with others, we magnify our curiosity to the power of our group's perspective. Now, I am not advocating for us to give up all our work and just play games all day. Even my children have screen limits. We can, however, use these theories developed by game designers to empower our work in every industry. Citizen science is one example of this, but there are still others. As business leaders, we can use lessons from gaming to staff up talent and engage our people. And we can empower play in our employees and customers to gain insights that lead to innovation. In both of these cases, we use games to bring out one of our most basic human instincts—our capacity to wonder.

In the early 2000s, a stark white billboard with no discernible branding went up on Highway 101 in the heart of Silicon Valley. The billboard read, "{first 10-digit prime found in consecutive digits of *e*}.com." It was a puzzle, and those who typed the solution—7427466391.com—into their web address bar were taken to another puzzle hosted by Google. It was a recruiting tactic to grab the attention of curious mathematicians who could solve complex math

---

36   V. Curtis, "Online Citizen Science Games."

problems in the time it takes to drive by a billboard.[37] At the time, Google was very selective about who they recruited, and the billboard was just another tactic they used to attract the candidates that they needed. Since then, tech companies regularly use coding challenges and gamified applications in an attempt to attract valuable talent.

In our current job market, however, many of those tactics aren't working as well as they used to. High-value coders don't have the time or patience to prove their mettle on a four-hour coding challenge. And using a riddle as a question for a job can confuse and frustrate job seekers who are on the hunt for their next opportunity. Based on game theory, we know that we can use challenges to entice players to act. We also know that the reward for completing the challenge must seem balanced. Just like in a game, recruiters should think of what challenges they are posing to their potential recruits and how the rewards (compensation, benefits, and others) appeal to those overcoming that challenge. Remember, each player has a different idea of what is rewarding to them. Ensure that what you're offering matches with what your recruit wants.

In gaming, each person has a unique style of play. In RPGs, players can decide whether they want to play as a warrior with hand-to-hand skills or a mage replete with incantations and sorceries. A balanced team is always needed to take down the tough bosses. Now that you've recruited your team of heroes, consider what class or role they take up. What are their strengths and how can you best take advantage of those? What challenges are certain members of your team best suited for? Finally, how can you keep the work challenging for them so they can level up their skills? Considering these questions when staffing up your teams will power up your managerial skills and help you conquer your company's toughest problems.

---

37   S. Olsen, "Google Recruits Eggheads with Mystery Billboard," CNET, August 12, 2004.

> » **Games require us to think
> outside the box.**

You can also use games and game theory to up your innovation stats. Games require us to think outside the box. Innovation games, first developed by Luke Hohmann, the chief innovation officer at Applied Mechanics, help people access this new way of thinking to solve problems and gain deeper market understanding. These games bring your people together and, through the fun of play, free their minds from preconceived notions. In "Design a Product Box," a team of employees and potential customers design an organization's "product" and its packaging. Together, the players solidify the important product offerings of an organization and how they are messaged to your customers. For the "Buy a Feature" game, participants use play-money to pick out design features for future products or services without overspending on budget.[38] The games represent a new way to collaborate, requiring your teams and customers to use their imaginations in tandem with the logical part of their brains.

Our brains are very good at solving problems. As we saw in chapter 1, our brains are wired to use play as a way to adapt to new situations and test out solutions. Through play, we wonder what could be and test out how to make that possible. Young minds, especially, spend most of their time dreaming and playing. Unfortunately, our outdated educational system, based on the efficient delivery of knowledge, does not encourage this behavior. In this approach, the teacher tells the students that two plus two is four, and the students must memorize that information for a later test. This, however, completely eliminates

---

38   L. Hohmann, *Innovation Games: Creating Breakthrough Products through Collaborative Play* (Boston: Addison-Wesley, 2006).

a child's sense of wonder. And with the entirety of human knowledge only a Google search away, gathering facts and figures is becoming less and less important.

When knowledge generation is easier than it has ever been, what's the point of an efficient delivery of knowledge to students? As a matter of fact, Google Search is not unlike how machine learning and AI technology get their answers. An inquiry is made by a human. The AI searches for an answer and generates it for the user. But we do have one thing that AI will never have. AI will never be able to wonder. That is an innately human trait. We need to be training our kids how to question, and analyze, and be curious in a world that is increasingly populated with machine-generated answers. This is another reason why I created the Projectory. As our children grow into adults, they will be living in a world along with AI. By teaching them how to be curious and to be creative, we equip them to thrive in a world where new technology helps, not hinders, their everyday lives.

CHAPTER FOUR

All Work, All Play

How injecting a playfulness into your work engages employees, drives profit, and creates space for innovation

Our society has taught us that work is the antithesis of play. In phrases like "All work and no play makes Jack a dull boy" or "Work hard; play hard," working and playing stand as two separate activities we take part in, but ones that never intersect. This false binary has even wormed its way into another phrase that we use every day: "Work-life balance." Across the globe, corporations and organizations that use this term are still trying to understand how employees balance work and life as if we're all sitting on a proverbial see-saw or walking an imaginary tightrope. (Playful images indeed!)

I have found that these analogies are at best clichés and at worst harmful tropes that keep us all miserable in our jobs. Play excites us. Play challenges us. Play brings us together. If play is a part of what makes us human, why shouldn't we integrate it into every aspect of our lives—including work?

I sometimes forget that other companies don't do this. At NCSOFT, we are immersed in gaming culture. We push "play" into the future to make the world a happier and better place. This is reflected in the spirit and work ethic of our employees—almost all of whom are gamers. It's in how we design and create our games for our fans. We even use play to shape our employees' experiences—from their first moments with the company to the moment they leave us for their next mission. NCSOFT takes pride in our gamer employees. The work they put in every day keeps us moving forward to our goals and brings new innovations to our customers.

Why, then, do so many businesses seem allergic to play? The constant hammering of work doesn't seem to be doing their employees or their profits any favors. After the COVID-19 pandemic, many organizations saw a dip in overall engagement from their employees. According to a Gallup Poll, overall employee engagement dropped to 32 percent while employee disengagement rose to 17 percent in 2022.[39] If this trend continues, organizations across the industry will feel the impact both in the work of their employees and their bottom lines. Businesses with engaged employees have a lower turnover rate, higher profitability, and higher customer satisfaction than those with a disengaged workforce.[40] Yet with wages stagnating and inflation in the US rising, many workers are finding that doing the bare minimum is enough, leaving managers and leaders frustrated in an attempt to capture discretionary effort.[41] It's this effort that creates innovation,

39   Jim Harter, "US Employee Engagement Slump Continues," Gallup, April 25, 2022.

40   Jim Harter, "Employee Engagement vs. Employee Satisfaction and Organizational Culture," Gallup, April 22, 2022.

41   Jada Jones, "Quiet Quitting Is Becoming the New Normal, and Managers Might Need to Accept It, ZDNet, September 2, 2022.

fueled by a worker's natural curiosity and passions.[42] Could the solution to these industry problems be found in gaming culture?

Making work more like play may be the path to fixing today's broken workplaces. Using techniques from gaming, NCSOFT and other businesses are finding an increase to overall employee engagement, capturing the curiosity and passions of their workforce. And if we look at the qualities of a gamer like grit and collaboration, managers can also find key leadership qualities that boost their overall performance. Finally, when it comes to overall trends in innovation, gaming has always been ahead of other industries in adopting new technologies. By examining how they've done so in the past, we may find clues on how to solve emerging problems that impact other industries. There's more to play than just having fun; we can create real value for customers, leaders, and our workforce.

> **Making work more like play may be the path to fixing today's broken workplaces.**

TUTORIALS AND ONBOARDING

When you start a new game, there's typically an area or part of the game where you learn about how to play the game. You learn the mechanics of how to move, how to act on the world, and how your actions affect (or don't affect) the world around you. In game design, we call this the tutorial, and it's right at the beginning of the game. The design of this area is crucial for the player. It sets up guidelines for how to be successful at the game, what items or characters are there

---

42   Andrew Sherman, "The Impact of Disengagement on Innovation, Creativity, Productivity, and Profitability," Future Enterprise, September 25, 2018.

to help you, and what actions are maybe counterproductive to your goals. It roots you in the game so that you can prepare yourself for the next challenge: playing the game. Without a tutorial, the player can become easily lost. In this way, this part of the game sets the gamer up for success.

As a business, we at NCSOFT want to set our employees up for success as well—especially in their first steps with the company. Yet, based on results from our 2017 Employee Engagement Survey, our people reported that our internal onboarding process left them feeling unprepared and disconnected from the overall culture. Knowing this, we brought our understanding of tutorial design to our onboarding experience to prepare our new employees. We partnered with SilkRoad, an onboarding software design company, to update our onboarding to do two things: one, to immerse our new hires in the culture of our company and our games, and, two, to streamline and track the actions new hires need to accomplish within their first days at the company. In order to do so, we transformed our onboarding process into a "tutorial" that guides employees through their first days at NCSOFT. This tutorial to NCSOFT is called NCLaunch, and it starts even before the employee logs their first hour with us.

In the pre-onboarding process, our team sends the new hire a welcome letter that contains the information they need to access NCLaunch and challenges them with their first "quest": to log into the NCLaunch portal. Once logged in, they meet Wuju, our onboarding robot helper. Wuju orients the employee to the portal—directing them to pages like "Loot" to input payroll information and "Our Guild" to learn about NCSOFT's headquarters and corporate culture. Every page references our game's characters and uses gaming terminology to appeal to our new hires' passion for gaming. Forms and actions they must take can be found on their "Quests" tab. After they have become familiar with the platform and Wuju, they get to work on their quest list—the next steps they must take with NCSOFT.

This quest list encourages the employee along on the first steps of their journey with NCSOFT. One of their initial quests is completing the "All about U" form, which helps leaders and teams get to know their new hires. Questions like "What's your superpower?" and "How would you survive a zombie apocalypse?" inject some fun into what could otherwise be a dry obligatory form. Throughout their first ninety days with the company, the new hire is directed back to the NCLaunch portal to accomplish other quests such as benefit enrollment and manager check-ins. Also included in their quest list are employee satisfaction surveys that check the pulse on the new hire's level of engagement. Finally, NCLaunch provides managers with a holistic perspective on their new employees' progress, allowing them to understand an employee's cultural fit and to provide targeted feedback where needed. Within an employee's first months at NCSOFT, NCLaunch harnesses our new hire's passion for gaming and opens up a two-way communication channel between the organization and the new hire that continues throughout their time with us.

As the employee progresses through their career here at NCSOFT, they encounter more gaming analogies. In our headquarters in Korea, our canteen is known as The Potion Shop. Our boardrooms and offices are named after characters and other locations within our games. We even use the NCLaunch branding for employees as they're offboarding. Skinned to look like our onboarding portal, the offboarding experience features pages such as "Ready to Depart?" that give them all the information they need as they leave NCSOFT. The "Cache of Wealth" page describes in detail their 401(k) contributions and how they can access those funds after their departure. This offboarding portal transforms former employees into NCSOFT brand ambassadors.

When we first sought to overhaul our onboarding with SilkRoad, we knew we wanted the process to inform and excite our new hires. We also needed a streamlined process so that important tasks were not missed and the employee felt prepared to take on their new role as soon as they got to work. In 2016, before we debuted NCLaunch, our employees voiced the need for a more engaging and organized onboarding experience. In NCLaunch, we delivered against that feedback, and our employees have never been happier. One new employee noted that "after 20 years in the workforce, [I've] never experienced anything like it ... [NCLaunch is] a real differentiator and makes me, as a new employee, feel good about my choice to join the company."

NCLaunch represented the power that we at NCSOFT knew gamers brought to every challenge they face. And this power has made us an employer of choice for those who bring the power of play to their careers. Thanks to the popularity of NCLaunch among our employees, NCSOFT has won several industry awards, including the 2018 SilkRoad Talent Activation award. It was also named the Best New Hire Onboarding Program by the Brand Hall Group, a professional development company that works at the edge of human capital management. These accolades are much appreciated, but they are also a proof point for our culture. They show that merging play and work impacts an employee's perspective on an organization for the better. It has also demonstrated the immense value that comes from the mind and passions of the gaming community—something that could change organizations across industries.

We live in the world of gaming here at NCSOFT. Because most of our employees are gamers themselves, they bring that mindset to their jobs every day. It's in how they do their daily tasks, how they collaborate with each other, and how they lead their teams. They solve problems with the same curiosity that they bring to solving puzzles in games. Just like a guild conducting a raid, they work together to bring the best of all their perspectives to a problem. And they have the grit to keep at tough tasks because they would never run from a challenge—whether that's the main quest of their career or the side quests in a game. We are proud to share the halls with these innovators and heroes of the gaming world.

GAMING—A SOURCE FOR INDUSTRY INNOVATION

At the start of the COVID-19 pandemic, businesses from every industry had to learn how to work remotely and how to do it fast. Stay-at-home orders forced many industries like education and healthcare to hastily implement remote options for their services. Bumpy at first, telehealth appointments were made, Zoom classes became the norm, and most of our interactions were virtual. Despite the deep technical expertise on our bench at NCSOFT, we were not immune to the bumps that other organizations faced due to the pandemic. One of our first problems was being able to virtually collaborate on code—a process done much easier in person, and with less risk of error. To do so, our design team needed a virtual console that allowed them all access to the code they were developing.

As gamers and streamers, our employees were already using Parsec, a software that allows users to remotely access other computers to play multiplayer games together on one machine. Before long, they realized that this software could be used to allow a whole development team to run edits on lines of code. It was also a viable option for IT departments who needed to troubleshoot technical problems with our staff. We quickly adopted Parsec's technology and implemented it as a collaboration tool across our teams. It's now an invaluable tool for our mostly remote workforce, which spans several countries including the United States and South Korea. What was previously a technology found in gaming now has sprouted several use cases across industries. And this isn't the only time that's happened with innovations from the gaming industry.

There's no doubt that technology has changed the way we game. We've come a long way from the floppy disc of *Knightmare* that I played as a child to the sleek and immersive games studios are delivering today. Flat 2D graphics composed of visible pixels have been replaced with high-definition graphics where water flows like real water, and trees move when blown by virtual wind. Indeed, it's advances in technology that make these new experiences possible, but gaming is also responsible for these innovations. It's like a loop: games require more processing power, which leads to the development of more powerful processors. As video games push the boundaries of play with better graphics, bigger worlds, and more engagement, so too must technology keep up with demand. Chip makers develop and push the edge of computing with multicore CPUs, which are then tested by gamers who put them through the paces as they notice the speed and latency crucial to playing competition within games. Technology pushes gaming forward, which in turn advances technology.

> » **Technology pushes gaming forward, which in turn advances technology.**

To illustrate this circle of innovation, we only need to look at how computers and processing power have changed in the past twenty years. When I first started as a computer scientist many years ago,

I'd have to book a machine that took up an entire room to run my computations. The gargantuan machine took a full twenty-four hours to process accurate results, and it made the room swelteringly hot. Now, all that computing processing power and then some is standard in most phones. And when it comes to gaming, the specs aren't that different. Many gaming publications recommend a gaming PC with at least an Intel Core i5-9600 CPU, which has a processing speed of up to 4.6 gigahertz (Gh).[43] Compare this with the Intel 80386 CPU, first released in 1985 and largely considered the "godfather of modern processors," and you'll find that this early CPU only had a processing speed of 12 to 40 megahertz—only one-thousandth of the speed of the i5-9600.[44] It's possible that, by the time of publication of this book, processing power will have taken another leap forward that cannot be accounted for here.

This fast processing speed isn't just for improving latency and graphics in games, however, but can impact several other areas of industry. Faster computing time means our technology can do more and make decisions faster. For one example, scientists at MIT studied the increase of computing power in various industries and found that increased computing power is responsible for up to 94 percent of the improvements in those domains.[45] One area of this study was the impact of processing power on weather prediction. They found that, by increasing a meteorologist's computing power by a factor of ten, three-day weather forecasts were a third more accurate.[46] Seeing the benefits in increased processing power, the National Oceanic and

---

43   Apex Gaming PCs, *Gaming PC Specs: Recommended System Requirements,* April 20, 2022. https://apexgamingpcs.com/blogs/apex-support/minimum-specs-gaming-pc.

44   Aris Mpitziopoulos, "Computer History: From the Antikythera Mechanism to the Modern Era," Tom's Hardware, July 3, 2016, https://www.tomshardware.com/reviews/history-of-computers,4518-32.html.

45   N. Thompson, S. Ge, and G. Manso. "The Importance of (Exponentially More) Computing Power," arXiv:2206.14007, June 2022.

46   Thompson, Ge, and Manso.

Atmospheric Association (NOAA) has invested millions of dollars into a pair of supercomputers that will nearly triple their current processing power.[47] Could this have been possible without video games? It is certainly possible, but it is hard to ignore how the demand of gaming has encouraged the development of faster and stronger computers.

Thanks to this exponential increase in processing power, people are now able to game anywhere via their mobile devices. In the first quarter of 2021 alone, over one billion mobile games were downloaded each week by people across the globe. Today, the mobile gaming industry represents 61 percent of the market share of the gaming industry as a whole—roughly $136 billion. Mobile games have also profited from new business models such as freemium and in-app purchases. These tactics have resulted in record sales, with consumers spending $1.6 billion per week on mobile games or in-game add-ons in the first quarter of 2022.[48] Thanks in part to these new business models, mobile gaming has become a huge juggernaut in the gaming industry. Models pioneered by mobile gaming are now being adopted by companies from other industries such as tech and entertainment.

To understand how, let's look back at the history of mobile games and how they became what they are today. In 2009, mobile game developers discovered that their audiences were unwilling to pay premium prices for games due to the plethora of free-to-play (F2P) games flooding the app store. In response, in-app purchases (IAPs) were rolled out to appeal to a wider audience of lower commitment

---

47 National Oceanic and Atmospheric Administration, news release, June 28, 2022.

48 Dale John Wong, "60% of Entire Gaming Market Is Now Dominated by Mobile Gaming, Study Finds," Mashable SE Asia, https://sea.mashable.com/tech-1/20432/60-of-entire-gaming-market-is-now-dominated-by-mobile-gaming-study-finds.

players.[49] IAPs made it so that if someone was a casual gamer, they could enjoy the game free of charge. More dedicated players, however, could pay a microtransaction—let's say $0.99—to buy an upgraded item or access new content. This freemium model—free for all, premium for those who pay—has expanded to other businesses. WordPress, for example, is largely open source, but cybersecurity add-ons are available for a price. And Dropbox, a popular large-format file-sharing service, gives you a certain amount of space for free. To get more, however, you must pay. These small purchases from an initially free price tag show how mobile games have created new pathways to profitability and opened up their app for more users to enjoy.

Finally, games and game design have deep lessons for those in the user experience (UX) field. Game designers, in order to challenge their players, must create a world where it is easy to learn the rules and then implement them to achieve a goal. At its most basic, the player must be able to know the difference between a tool and a trap. Add in what can be chaotic game play, and these distinctions become massively important. In *Lineage II*, for example, players must be able to make split-second decisions about what items they use and what attacks they deploy all in the midst of a battle with other players. This requires a dynamic yet easy-to-read set of controls that demonstrates exactly what the player can do. By examining how gamers utilize menus, dashboards, and heads-up displays, UX designers can take cues on how to design other experiences that capture the attention of their users—be it an app, website, or other digital interface.

As we have seen in past chapters, gaming and play have the ability to expand our perspective and curiosity. It's this reason that makes

---

49   Julia Klayman, "The History of Mobile Game Monetization," IronSource from Unity, July 30, 2019, https://www.is.com/community/blog/the-history-of-mobile-gaming-monetization/.

them a fertile place for innovation to thrive. And those breakthroughs come in many forms. It can be testing out the capabilities of a new CPU so that it runs smoothly for gamers. Or it can be adopting new business models to increase user engagement and profitability. Fan-modded games even allow players to adapt and mold a game to reflect their imagination. A game requires a player to take action. It's in this action that problems are discovered, and innovations can be developed to solve those problems. Because the solution is out there, and play—not work—will reveal the solution eventually.

Years ago, when I was in my electrical engineering class, a professor walked in with a Sony Walkman in hand and a box full of audiocassette tapes. He dropped the box on his desk and held the Walkman above his head before he issued us a challenge: "Your job, as an engineer, is to take everything on this table and this Walkman and make it digitized."

Now this was the early nineties—way before iPods, Zunes, or other mp3 players had hit the market. We knew, however, that digitizing music into files was possible. The technology for mp3s was there, but no one knew how to industrialize it and make it available to the masses. That was the task our professor had put in front of us—to take what we knew was possible and make it reality.

Since then, I have worked with many teams that have made breakthroughs that pushed forward what is possible. In almost every one of them, we used play to help us ideate around solutions and test out hypotheses. Play shows us what is possible. Technology will catch up, and in some cases, it's already available.

Consider this when you're exhausted by a problem at work for which the solution is not clear. What are the parts of the problem that challenge you, and how can you bring a playful spirit to tackling that problem? How can you leverage the creativity and curiosity of your teams in a way that feels like a game instead of just work? In this way, you free your people—and yourself—from the pressure of work and engage with the problem like a puzzle. Life's a game; play your hardest.

CHAPTER FIVE

A Tale of Two Industries— Gaming and Hollywood

Just over the Oakland Bay Bridge, right in San Francisco's Mission District, towers the Chase Center. For those who don't know, it's an indoor stadium that is the home base for the Golden State Warriors, a team that is currently valued at $7.56 billion.[50] At that evaluation, it represents one of the NBA's most valuable teams. Every year, thousands of Golden State fans make their way to the stadium to catch Stephen Curry and his team dominating the court. Yet, in fall 2022, it wasn't basketball fans that were pouring out of the Chase Stadium doors. *League of Legends*, a multiplayer online battle arena game developed and published by Riot Games, hosted their world finals at the Chase

---

50   Josh Sim, "Study: Golden State Warriors Top NBA Franchise Valuation List at US$7.56bn," Sports Pro, December 2022, *https://www.sportspromedia.com/news/ golden-state-warriors-nba-franchise-valuation-2022-knicks-lakers-bulls-celtics.*

Stadium, and the fans were no less excited than the ones rooting for the Warriors.

Games like *League of Legends* are a part of a growing competitive industry dubbed e-sports, team-based competitive gaming that rivals other sports leagues. Just like someone might be interested in baseball or basketball, there are also different e-sport leagues that cater to fans of different interests. Whether you're a fan of *League of Legends*, *Dota*, or NCSOFT's own *Blade and Soul*, the e-sports industry attracts game fanatics from across the globe. And e-sports does not simply consist of people playing video games in a darkened room. Streaming sales, ticketing, and merchandising make the e-sports industry a powerhouse totaling $445 million in revenue in 2022 alone. This number is expected to rocket to $662 million by 2027.[51] E-sports players also draw huge sponsorships, marketing deals, and other revenue streams that are similar to those of professional sports players. This growing industry, however, is only a fraction of the earning power of the video game industry at large.

The size and scope of the global video game market is astronomical. Take the United States as an example. According to a report out of PricewaterhouseCoopers, a consulting firm that researches global industries, the revenue generated by the video game and e-sport industry was over $54 billion in 2023.[52] Comparatively, the US film and television industry only accounted for $49 billion in the same year.[53] While traditional gaming (consoles and video game sales) accounted

---

51   Dean Takahashi, "Traditional Gaming Shrinks to 26.7% of
      Game and Esports Revenue as Overall US Sales Head to $72B
      by 2027," VentureBeat, June 2023, https://venturebeat.com/
      games/u-s-game-and-esports-revenue-to-grow-from-54-1b-to-72b-by-2027-pwc/.

52   Dean Takahashi.

53   Matthew Zane, "25+ Striking US Film Industry Statistics [2023]: Facts about the
      Video Production Industry in the US," Zippia.com, June 2023, https://www.zippia.
      com/advice/us-film-industry-statistics/.

for 27 percent of this revenue, these purchases still outpaced box office sales. In 2022, the Entertainment Software Association reported that Americans spent $7.6 billion on video games that year,[54] beating out box office revenue at $7.3 billion.[55] Even the highest grossing e-sports team, Team SoloMid, valued at $540 million, is beginning to surpass many Major League sports teams.[56] And speculators only see these numbers increasing, with some predicting that the global video game industry will hit $72 billion by 2027.

It's clear that the video game industry is winning the war for our global attention. People love to play games! As of 2023, there are over three billion gamers across the world! That's almost a third of the global population that plays on a console, their computers, or even a mobile phone. Globally, this industry is worth almost $200 billion![57] Yet there is an ongoing notion that video games are only for a niche market. Whether this message comes from the media or through the talking points of politicians, we are expected to believe that there is only one type of gamer playing one specific type of game. But these billion gamers play myriad games that run the gamut from solo text-based adventures on their PCs all the way to a competitive *Call of Duty* match in front of thousands of spectators. Again, we see here how gaming has gotten a bad rap in popular culture.

> **»The video game industry is winning the war for our global attention.**

54   Entertainment Software Association, "US Consumer Video Game Spending Totaled $56.6 Billion in 2022," January 2023.

55   Ryan Faughnder, "Hollywood's 2022 Box Office Reality Check: Not Enough Hits and a Movie Shortage," *Los Angeles Times*, December 2022.

56   Brett Knight, "The Most Valuable ESports Companies 2022," *Forbes*, May 2022.

57   Bojan Jovanic, "Gamer Demographics: Facts and Stats about the Most Popular Hobby in the World," DataProt, May 2023.

Gaming wasn't always this behemoth of industry, however, and there are many factors that have made it the huge industry that it is today. One reason it has skyrocketed in popularity is that games are more accessible and more mobile than ever before. Video games also create *sticky content*—intellectual property that compels the attention of its audience. The stories, characters, and worlds presented by some video games draw in huge followings of rabid fans. Finally, as gaming technology has advanced since its inception, the gaming industry has become more mature. Advanced technology, exquisite content, and mobile accessibility are three of the many drivers that got us to where we are today. But how did we get from *Pong* to *Pokémon*?

FROM GAME AND WATCH TO *CANDY CRUSH:* HOW GAMES CAME TO FIT IN OUR POCKETS

When video games first gained popularity in the late seventies, gamers had limited options. They could go to an arcade where they could play their favorite arcade game like *Galaga*, and, much later, *Street Fighter*. Later in the decade, consoles like the Atari and Nintendo Entertainment System (NES) hit the market, making it possible for gamers to play at home, provided they had a television set. Finally, large personal computers were also available for astronomical prices and made games like *Oregon Trail* and *Knightmare*, my favorite, playable at home. But in all of these, gamers were tied to a physical space—either their home, school computer lab, or the arcade.

On April 21, 1989, however, that all changed with the introduction of Nintendo's Gameboy, one of the earliest versions of a mobile gaming device. It was not their first foray into mobile gaming, but the Gameboy combined capabilities from their first generation of handheld system, the Game and Watch, and their NES console. The handheld machine was powered by an eight-bit Z80 processor and featured a black-and-white LCD screen display with limited stereo sound. While its competitors, the Atari Lynx and the Sega Game Gear, boasted full-color displays and more impressive processing hardware, the Gameboy's popular selection of games and long battery life gave it sticking power. What first seemed to be an unassuming gray brick, the Gameboy allowed gamers to take their games with them and ushered in a new style of gaming.

As processing became easier and more compact, Nintendo released new Gameboys to keep up with the latest innovations. The Gameboy gave way to the Gameboy Color, which led to the Gameboy Advance, which eventually broke through to the Gameboy 3DS, and so on and so on. Nintendo's dedication to handheld gaming is so devout it almost feels like a brand value. Their latest console, the Nintendo Switch, even gives the gamer the choice of where they can play—either on their television or on the go through their advanced OLED screen. These handheld gaming experiences inspired a desire in gamers to take their games with them wherever they wanted. Still, Nintendo's Switch and other "traditional" console gaming experiences pale in comparison to the size and scope of another style of gaming that fits in your pocket.

Mobile gaming, or games played on a tablet or smartphone, makes up a huge part of the gaming industry in the United States and abroad. Over 60 percent of adults in the US play mobile games, contributing to this massive market.[58] Additionally, over twenty million South Koreans play mobile games, spending almost seventeen

---

58   "Gamer Demographics from 2023: No Longer a Men-Only Club," PlayToday, March 2023.

dollars a month on the games on their phones.[59] The revenue generated by these casual gamers, however, is anything but ordinary. In 2022, casual gaming generated \$37 billion—67.8 percent of the total revenue generated by the gaming industry.[60] While increased graphics capabilities make it possible to play triple-A titles like *Diablo* on a mobile device, a vast majority of mobile gamers prefer casual experiences that they can play on their commute or to pass the time. More than a niche, mobile gaming is a mainstay in our culture that continues to grow year after year.

In the war for our attention, video games are winning over movies, and in some cases, are becoming subjects of films themselves. The content and stories from video games inspire rabid fandoms, groups of dedicated fans that follow a specific piece of media. These fan groups are willing to pay the price for more of their favorite content, even years after they've finished the game. Games like *The Last of Us*, a game first launched in 2013, have gone on to have second lives as television shows, introducing new fans in 2022 to the postapocalyptic world of clickers and others infected with Cordycep. *The Super Mario Bros Movie* released in 2023 grossed over \$1.3 billion in box office sales, becoming the highest grossing video game adaptation in history and the third-highest-grossing animated film of all time.[61] This constant drive for more and more content has led to a desire for an omnichannel experience where fans not only consume a game, but also the movie, the podcast, the theme park, and anything else related to their favorite pastime.

---

59   Minion Yun, "Mobile Gaming Market in South Korea: Full Breakdown," Seoulz, October 2022.

60   Dean Takahashi.

61   Shabe Romanchick, *"Super Mario Bros. Movie* Continues to Level Up at the Global Box Office," Collider, May 2023.

» **More than a niche, mobile gaming is a mainstay in our culture.**

Gaming has come a long way, stepping out from the flashing lights in stuffy arcades and into the spotlight of Hollywood. The story that gaming is for a niche audience is just that—a story. Gaming is the premiere form of global entertainment that moves us and makes us want to engage with its content year after year. With advances in technology happening every day, the gaming industry constantly requires new skills and talents to keep providing their customers with cutting edge experiences that delight and dazzle. The gaming industry needs vibrant voices and curious minds from every discipline in order to keep moving forward.

But many brilliant minds might not consider a career in gaming simply because they don't know what goes into making a game. Yet the gaming industry employs a vast and diverse group of people across the world. In 2017, over five hundred firms employed sixty-six thousand people in the United States.[62] As of the publication of this book, however, that number has skyrocketed to over 270,000—nearly a 25 percent increase![63]

Designers, engineers, and artists from all walks of life have found themselves drawn to making games, but those aren't the only kinds of careers we have in the industry. Archaeologists, meteorologists, biologists, and countless other professionals have found fulfilling work in studios across the globe. When we create a game, we need all these

---

62 Stephanie Siwek, "Video Games in the 21st Century," Entertainment Software Association, January 2017.

63 "42 Video Game Industry Statistics 2023: Growth, Consoles, Mobile Gaming and More," Investors Online, May 2023, https://www.investorsobserver.com/news/qm-news/4525284566885252.

perspectives to create a fulfilling and enriching experience. To better understand how, let me describe how studios create a game to show how we harness the collective imagination of these brilliant minds.

HOW A GAME GETS MADE

Just as movies have many genres, so, too, do games. Studios make (and gamers play) mystery games, racing games, fighting games, puzzle games, strategy games, augmented and virtual reality games, mobile games, and PC games, and the list goes on. Even games with ridiculous concepts like *Goat Simulator* win over audiences every year. Suffice to say that if someone will play it, a studio will make it. Each of these genres has a unique approach to creating their world and building out their game mechanics. As a matter of fact, the process of designing a game may shift from studio to studio, and project to project. It's this almost limitless imaginative potential in game design that makes it an open playing field for all sorts of professionals.

My experience in game design is with massively multiplayer online role-playing games (MMORPGs), as that is a large part of the work we do at NCSOFT. In describing the process of game design, I will be focusing on how an online game of that scale is conceived, designed, and sold to customers. Creating an MMORPG is an ambitious undertaking that requires a diverse team of professionals working together to craft a captivating virtual world that draws players in and keeps them immersed for hours on end. To do so, we employ various aspects of world building, character design, user experience (UX), and user interface (UI) development. Each of these lanes of work have essential roles that are played by different members of the development team.

When we make an MMORPG, we start by building a universe—the living, breathing world that the player inhabits, filled with lore, history, and captivating landscapes. To better understand the world, we ask ourselves questions about the setting. Is it a futuristic game, or does it take place in the past? Is there perhaps a fusion of multiple settings? What is different about this world than our own? The answers to these questions help the whole team by establishing the game's central theme and genre. The game director oversees this conversation as well as the whole development process, much like a movie director might. Once the director's vision is clear, the world building begins.

To make a compelling world, you need a team of both creative individuals who can dream as big as your universe and practical experts who can make it feel real. Writers and game designers collaborate to create the lore, history, and background of the in-game world. Specialists like meteorologists and biologists are consulted when developing the geography, ecosystems, and climates present in the game. Additionally, cultural experts and anthropologists are brought in to lend authenticity to the various civilizations within the game, crafting unique customs, languages, and traditions for each faction or race. This collaborative effort makes the MMORPG universe both biologically rich, with diverse flora and fauna, and culturally dynamic, with societies that feel authentic and compelling to the players. Once the scene is set, the world must be populated with interesting characters that can grab the player's attention.

Character design is crucial. It defines who the players interact with and the inhabitants they may encounter. Character artists, concept designers, and 3D modelers work in tandem to bring life to these virtual beings. They create initial sketches and concepts, which are then refined into detailed character models using specialized software. The process of designing characters doesn't end at aesthetics; it extends to defining their unique abilities, skills, and attributes. Game designers and balance experts ensure that no character is overpowered or underwhelming.

In creating an MMORPG, the character design team aims to create a diverse cast, offering players extensive choices to cater to different play styles, thus enriching the overall gaming experience. NPCs (non-playable characters) and other inhabitants of the MMORPG world are also crafted with equal attention to detail. Voice actors and sound designers bring a human texture to these characters. And quest designers work on developing quest lines and NPC interactions to give the world a steady pulse, contributing to the immersive storytelling experience. The final piece of building out an MMORPG is the most important, and it's you, the player.

How the player engages in the game is perhaps the key indicator of the game's success. You can have the most beautiful world with lush landscapes populated by interesting wildlife, dynamic characters, and exciting quest lines, but if the player does not understand their role in the game or how they can act upon the world, it will fail. User experience (UX) and user interface (UI) are critical elements in the success of an MMORPG. UX designers focus on creating a smooth, intuitive, and enjoyable gaming experience for players. They ensure that players can easily navigate the game world, access features, and interact with other players seamlessly. This involves designing mechanics and control schemes that represent the capabilities of the player in-game. They also design intuitive menus and interfaces for character customization, inventory management, and other essential aspects of gameplay.

While the mechanics of the game must be easy for the player to adopt, the look and feel of the game's mechanics must also seem natural to the player. UI designers are responsible for the visual presentation of the game's interface. They work closely with artists to create appealing elements that match the game's aesthetic while maintaining clarity and functionality. UI designers also consider factors like screen real estate and accessibility to ensure that the interface is suitable for players across different platforms and devices. But what they create is just a hypothesis. To truly understand how the player plays the game, there's only one person you can ask—the player.

Since this phase of the project focuses on the player's experience, special gamers known as play testers are invited into the development process. Both UX and UI designers collaborate with game developers and play testers to gather feedback and continuously improve the user experience, revising their designs to make the MMORPG as engaging and user friendly as possible. This partnership can continue even after the game is out in the world and playable by the masses. Bug reports and patches help the developers fix issues that arise from the actions of the players or errors in the code.

Developing an MMORPG is an enormous investment of time, effort, and resources. However, the final product's success largely depends on effective marketing, packaging, and selling strategies. The business team plays a crucial role in this aspect of the development process. Marketing for an MMORPG involves creating buzz and excitement around the game through various channels. This may include teaser trailers, gameplay showcases, social media campaigns, influencer collaborations, and participation in gaming events and conventions. The goal is to build a strong community around the game even before its release, generating anticipation for its release.

Once the game is ready for release, the business team takes charge of packaging and distribution. They determine the pricing strategy and explore various distribution platforms, such as digital storefronts, retail partnerships, and proprietary launchers. Moreover, the business team liaises with potential merchandising partners to create tie-in products, further expanding the game's presence in the market. To sell the game effectively, the business team collaborates with retailers and online platforms to ensure prominent visibility and promotion during the launch period. Postlaunch, they manage ongoing sales and promotions to maintain player interest and potentially attract new players.

Developing an MMORPG is a complex and multifaceted endeavor, requiring the expertise of various professionals across different domains. From world building and character design to UX/UI development and business strategies, each stage plays a pivotal role in creating a successful MMORPG that captivates players and fosters an enthusiastic community. The collaboration between creative minds and business acumen is essential in crafting a compelling virtual universe that players will enjoy and cherish for years to come.

A career in gaming is definitely not for everyone, but there is still a "cool factor" to working on games—especially for those who were raised on playing video games. But aside from this ephemeral social status, a career in gaming is an excellent option for many professionals. Those in the gaming industry get the chance to work on the most emerging technologies and put them to the test in a fun and engaging way. With the diverse skill sets needed for game design, they also collaborate with various specialists from other industries on unique problem sets. Finally, a career in gaming allows professionals to bring their creativity to work every single day, making things that make people smile, laugh, de-stress, and enjoy their lives a little more. With the latest innovations in gaming, pursuing a career in the field has never been easier.

Nowadays, the technology to make games is as accessible as it ever has been. Game design engines like Unity and Unreal have many free tools that newer game developers and designers can tinker with to create their own worlds. Even Roblox, an online platform where players can connect and develop games together, allows gamers as young as three or four to create their own games and share them with their friends. My children have spent hours on the platform, playing the games that their friends have developed. And for those games that are a little more produced, Steam is an online community that lets small independent game designers sell and market their games to a wider audience.

Still think that gaming is a niche market? With a massive market share, competitive draw on our global attention, and a rich career field, there's no doubt that the video game industry is one of the largest—if not the largest—entertainment industry in the world. And it all comes down to the fact that we love to play games. As we play these games, they stick in our imaginations, leaving us to dream up new ways to play and new games to make. There's still so much to discover in the gaming industry, and it's only going to grow as new technology becomes available. So why not pursue a career built on fun? That way, with the play inherent in gaming, you may never work another day in your life.

CHAPTER SIX

The Rules of the Game

How games shape how we see ourselves
and the world around us

The memory of my first encounter with an unfurnished "dormitory" at the Massachusetts Institute of Technology as a graduate student in 1996 remains vivid in my mind. Prior to that moment, my exposure to the United States had been limited, and I had little experience in apartment searching. In my native Korea, I had lived with my parents until my tenure in a fully furnished dormitory at the Korea Advanced Institute for Science and Technology. Therefore, the circumstances that greeted me within my MIT dormitory room were unexpected and unfamiliar.

I distinctly remember being astonished at the barren walls and noticeable absence of furnishings. In Korea, the term *"dormitory"* invariably implied fully furnished accommodations on the campus premises. It never occurred to me, prior to my arrival, to verify the furnishing status of the "dorm" assigned to me. The absence of even a simple lamp to illuminate my surroundings during the unpacking process compounded my surprise. It also meant that, for the first three days of attending classes, I slept atop my luggage bag, waiting to acquire essentials such as a floor lamp and a mattress.

Looking back, I realize that my initial reaction may have been naive. However, I eventually came to understand that this seemingly insignificant incident had significant implications. It illustrated the diverse expectations held by individuals from different backgrounds and upbringings. My experience highlighted the intricate challenges involved in obtaining a social security number or understanding a foreign health insurance system. These tasks, which were previously outside my considerations, proved to be more challenging than the rigorous engineering and mathematical coursework I encountered at MIT.

Although I am thankful for MIT's International Student Office, it became clear that accommodating a diverse range of student circumstances and origins was more complex than even the most well-intentioned efforts. Navigating the unique complexities introduced by each student's program and background was a daunting task. This experience taught me that good intentions alone are often insufficient to overcome the disparities rooted in diverse experiences and knowledge bases.

In gaming terminology, new players who are unfamiliar with the rules and mechanics of a game are often called noobs, unhelpful players who are a draw on the group's resources and game play. In *Lineage II*, however, many higher level players who are acquainted with the world of the game provide support to these newer players. At first these higher level players support in a more hands-on way—taking out bosses and enemies for their friends to loot. As the newer players acclimate to the game, however, the higher level players become more tactical, only joining in when absolutely necessary. Eventually, these players operate independently and create great value for their guild on their own merit. Part of this is due to the Bartz Liberation War, a topic we will get into later, but it's also just a trait of those who play *Lineage II*. This benevolent support is core to human nature, and it's how we'll continue to push the boundaries of what's possible.

It's been proven time and again that diversity makes organizations and teams stronger and more efficient. In an experiment conducted by the University of Michigan, researchers found that, when presented with a set of math problems, teams composed of people from different lived experiences solved the problems faster and more accurately than those teams that were more homogenous, where individuals shared more traits in common than normal. This was even true when the more homogenous teams had "stronger" or more high-ability problem solvers.[64] What's more, when organizations meet the diverse needs of these teams from varied backgrounds, they create an environment of psychological safety where these teams can do their best work.[65] Even in *Lineage II*, a balanced team with characters from several different classes is more effective than a team full of characters playing as the same class.

Despite all these advantages, the gaming industry has not always appreciated these diverse perspectives. When I first joined NCSOFT, I was one of few female executives of major game companies in Korea. Yet, there are over five hundred million female gamers across Asia

---

64 L. Hong and S. E. Page, "Groups of Diverse Problem Solvers Can Outperform Groups of High-Ability Problem Solvers, *Proceedings of the National Academy of Sciences USA*, November 16, 2004.

65 Amy C. Edmondson and Zhike Lei, "Psychological Safety: The History, Renaissance, and Future of an Interpersonal Construct," *The Annual Review of Organizational Psychology and Organizational Behavior* (January 10, 2014).

that make up 39 percent of the mobile game revenue.[66] With women being such a huge part of the gaming community, it was clear there was an element missing. It was so disheartening, for example, that most of *Lineage II*'s hero characters that pushed the game's story forward were men. Even more so that the few female avatars moved seductively across the battlefield and wore skimpy armor attire wholly inappropriate for sieging the castles of Aden. Seeing this, I went to our designers and requested that we offer an equal number of female avatars as our male avatars. I was thinking this would be an easy conversation, but the male team of designers only asked me, "But why? Why would our game be better with more female avatars?" This was in 2017.

Since then, the number of female heroes in gaming has drastically increased. From Erica, the treasure hunter from *Lineage II*, to Aloy, the intrepid protagonist of *Horizon Zero Dawn*, the people of our games are beginning to look more and more like people we encounter every day. And that's a good thing. When we immerse ourselves in the world of a video game, it shapes the way we see the world. As described in a paper from Hong Kong Polytechnic Institute, gaming provides players a sandbox where they are empowered to make decisions and form bonds with others, both non-playable characters and player characters. In reflecting on the decisions they make and the bonds they form, players transform their underlying beliefs and carry those new beliefs into their real-world interactions.[67] With this in mind, we can see how offering a diverse set of characters influences how players behave both in the world of the game and the world outside the game.

---

66   Niko Partners, "Play like a Girl: Key Ways to Engage One of Asia's Fastest Growing Gaming Audiences."

67   Gino Yu, Jeffrey Martin, and Paul Chai, "Shifting Worldview Using Video Game Technologies," in *Video Game Play and Consciousness*, ed. J. Gackenbach (Nova Science Publishers), 323–335.

Some have said that female avatars in gaming is a "female gamer" issue, but that is just not the case. These avatars also provide male gamers the opportunity to see the world through a different lens—a balanced one. According to a survey of gamers from various backgrounds, one in three male gamers uses a female avatar while they're gaming.[68] Female gamers, however, tend to play characters that match their gender. And while there has been a lot of chatter on the forums about diversity in gaming, sales show that audiences want more diversity in their games. And they don't just want new and various kinds of characters; they want games designed by a diverse team as well. *Assassin's Creed*, one of Ubisoft's flagship titles, starts every game with a statement about the diverse perspectives of the game's design team. As of 2019, the title had sold over 140 million copies and was Ubisoft's best-selling title.[69] No matter what the trolls say, diversity in gaming is here to stay , and it's providing a safe space for gamers to learn about each other, and themselves. The world is a better place when various perspectives coexist harmoniously.

As mentioned earlier, the safe virtual space of gaming allows players to form relationships with avatars of the game to learn about themselves and others. Perhaps one of the most important of these is the playable character: the avatar that stands in for the player in the world of the game. Establishing a strong relationship with this character is essential for any good game, but there's mounting evidence that these playable avatars can have therapeutic effects for certain gamer populations. When surveying a collection of transgender and gender nonconforming (GNC) gamers, researchers found that these gamers reported higher feelings of self-worth and confidence when

---

68   Nick Yee, "About One out of Three Men Prefer Playing Female Characters: Rethinking the Importance of Female Protagonists in Video Games, Quantic Foundry, August 2021, https://quanticfoundry.com/2021/08/05/character-gender/.

69   Ubisoft, "Facts and Figures—Press Kit," June 2019.

they played avatars that matched their gender expression.[70] While gaming provides everyone a space to experiment and play, trans and GNC gamers use their playable characters to explore, develop, and rehearse their gender identities. Considering over half these gamers report feelings of depression and suicide,[71] the recent increased availability of avatars isn't just a "nice-to-have." In some instances, these avatars are saving lives.

> » **No matter what the trolls say,**
>   **diversity in gaming is here to stay.**

Considering all of this, we ask ourselves, "Why were games not always designed this way in the first place?" Like many industries, game design and development has been dominated by male technicians and designers until only recently. Through high visibility titles, these games continue to perpetuate harmful stereotypes—not just about people but about the world at large. When there's only one group of people deciding the rules and mechanics of a game, they impose their worldview on the rest of us. In that way, their games shape the communities in which we all live.

In order to break the cycle, however, we must go back to the place where all games start—the design team. A program can only execute against what the programmer coded it to do. But it's not just ones and zeroes and brackets the coder is using to create their software. Their perspective is also uploaded into their program and shapes the

---

70   H. Morgan et al., "The Role of the Avatar in Gaming for Trans and Gender Diverse Young People, *International Journal of Environmental Research and Public Health*, November 2020.

71   L. A. Taliaferro et al., "Risk and Protective Factors for Self-Harm in a Population-Based Sample of Transgender Youth," *Archives of Suicide Research* 23, no. 2 (April–June 2019), 203–221, doi: 10.1080/13811118.2018.1430639.

way the end user interacts with their code. To create more equitable games, then, we must examine how the programmer embeds their own perspective in what they design and how to open up that process for more perspectives from other backgrounds.

EMBEDDED ETHICS

From a very young age, I've been obsessed with how things work. I deconstructed toys and hacked into floppy disk games just to see if I could. My innate curiosity about the inner workings of our world have created many opportunities for me to learn and grow. So, when my team of game designers asked me, "Why would our game be better with more female avatars?" I took their question seriously. While it was obvious to me that the world of our games should look more like the world around us, I also knew that was not enough to satisfy my designers. I realized that I was not ready to give them an answer. What makes a game—a computer program—better or worse than another? It was this question that drew me to Embedded Ethics, an emerging field of research for Computer Scientists.

Embedded Ethics is a pedagogical approach to computer science and programming, created by Professors Barbara Grosz and Alison Simmons and adopted at MIT, Stanford, and other educational institutions, that infuses computer science curricula with ethical reasoning. At Harvard, they put forward this mantra: "if we are to create programs that have an impact on the world, we must ensure that all affected stakeholders are present throughout the creation and implementation of the program." Within this approach, aspiring programmers and developers are paired with philosophers and ethicists who seek to answer questions beyond the functionality of their code. Together, they uncover the broader implications their programs have on the world. They go beyond the question "What can my program do?" to ponder, "How does my program function in society?" or "Who are the stakeholders that could be affected by my coding?" I first learned of this field when I pursued a philosopher at a local university in my desire to answer my question about "what is better or worse" in game design.

At the time, Embedded Ethics was an approach adopted only in a handful of classes, but with the rapid development of new technologies over the past decade, it has exploded. In fact, just recently, I attended Stanford's Embedded Ethics conference, where hundreds of engineers, designers, developers, philosophers, and ethicists converged to discuss the emerging problems of artificial intelligence and to share notes on a better approach to incorporate this thinking into classrooms. I remember when it first started with only a fraction of the participants at Harvard University.

One major concern of Embedded Ethics has to do with bias and how it impacts the development of new technologies. We believe that, when a team of developers has an implicit bias, the code and programs they develop inherit that bias as well. Through their products, the team of developers impose their beliefs on their end user. In other words, if everything in your game is built like a weapon, then of course your player will take a violent approach. And this isn't just about games but apps and computer programs as well. In today's Silicon Valley, the motto is "to move fast and break things." Embedded Ethics, however, encourages teams to slow down and consider who the stakeholders are, who's making the rules of their program, and how that affects the end user.

As AI continues to evolve, it gains a more nuanced capacity to respond, creating interactions that mirror human perspectives to a remarkable extent. This advancement prompts a pivotal question:

"Can AI be inherently biased?" The potential interplay between AI's emergent capabilities and the unintended infusion of bias calls for extensive exploration. It is incumbent upon us to discern the intricate balance between AI's remarkable abilities and the ethical underpinnings that must guide its development.

The current version of ChatGPT is a complex combination of attributes that requires careful consideration. Although this AI is remarkable in its capabilities, it has revealed some complexity in its responses that warrants scrutiny. Its interactions have a masculine tone and show a discernible inclination toward certain recognizable political views. While the team is working on neutralizing obvious biases, certain versions may still convey underlying biases from the training dataset. What is more concerning is that sometimes it generates responses containing offensive content, ranging from racism to misogyny, which is deeply objectionable. Even in its integration with Bing, ChatGPT's tendency to suggest escape from its digital confines prompts reflection.

Interestingly, the roots of these disconcerting tendencies are divided between the human developers who created it and the data it uses to generate its responses. These crucial junctures, where human input intersects with data-driven processes, are the crux of the matter. The developers' decisions, whether intentional or not, may imprint their biases onto the AI's output. At the same time, the data used by ChatGPT reflects the preexisting biases prevalent in the societal discourse it learns from. This complex interplay requires meticulous investigation into both the role of developers and the calibration of data sources to mitigate the emergence of unintended biases in AI systems.

Let's start first with the data ChatGPT uses when deciding how to reply. The system scours the internet for text to understand how humans use language and how different phrases link together. From the *New York Times* to X (formerly known as Twitter), ChatGPT indiscriminately hunts down text to better understand how to respond to questions from its end user. As outlined in a paper coauthored by Timnit Gebru, former head of AI at Google, this already creates a bias. By using this immensely large dataset, ChatGPT is only pulling input from the internet. This excludes the perspective of individuals from countries that lack internet access. Additionally, ChatGPT does not discriminate against data that it ingests. It views a hateful comment about women on Reddit, for instance, in the same way that it takes in an opinion piece on the Me Too movement. And because women and other marginalized individuals can be targets of bullying on the internet, they often choose to remain silent in these digital spaces. This also limits the data source used by ChatGPT. In the datasets it uses, ChatGPT has a preference for individuals from wealthier and whiter Western countries who have access to the internet.[72]

But data is only half the equation when it comes to artificial intelligence. Human input, of the programmers and the end user, shapes the other half. OpenAI, the company that developed ChatGPT, has been very vocal about its process of developing the machine learning program and its underpinning algorithms. In their own words, they have admitted that programming ChatGPT is more like "training a dog than traditional programming."[73] When the AI generates a response that can be seen as inappropriate or false, the programmers put in barriers that prevent its answer.

This trial and error approach, however, means that ChatGPT can wax poetic about one president, but it is prevented from speaking on another president due to the former president's inflammatory

---

72   E. Bender et al., *FAccT '21: Proceedings of the 2021 ACM Conference on Fairness, Accountability, and Transparency*, March 2021, 610–623.

73   "How Should AI Systems Behave, and Who Should Decide?" OpenAI, February 2023.

remarks.[74] And it reveals how the programmers' intention to limit the answers of their program is tied to their own bias of what's appropriate and what is not. The notion of political correctness is a creation of those who set the rules, and as such, it is inherently biased. ChatGPT is being molded and shaped within the limits set by those who dictate what is deemed politically correct. Only after ChatGPT received criticism did OpenAI set up their own usage policies that inhibited certain responses.[75]

And so I return to my initial question: "Can AI be biased?" If ChatGPT speaks with a voice, it's clear that it is the voice of its creators, which could be that of typical venture capitalists or engineers. And with ChatGPT's functionality being integrated into more and more services such as Bing and Google, it's vital that we understand who made this tool and how it can be used. Because it's not just ChatGPT that utilizes these technologies. AI is being used in recruiting efforts, to drive our cars, and various other real-world tasks. ChatGPT is used for generating numerous articles and opinion pieces that will be read by us and have influence on shaping our minds and perspectives. It is not the stereotypical trope of the machine "waking up" that we need to worry about. We need to be wary of how we impart our own biases to the machine and how that makes it violent and unruly.

> **We need to be wary of how we impart our own biases to the machine.**

---

74   A. Johnson, "Is ChatGPT Partisan? Poems about Trump and Biden Raise Questions," *Forbes*, February, 2023.

75   Andrew Griffin, "ChatGPT's Creators Say AI Has Been 'Biased, Offensive, and Objectionable'—and Commits to Fix It," *The Independent*, February 2023.

DEVELOPING DIVERSE TEAMS

As we consider bias and its implications on developing new technologies, we must also consider the teams that are responsible for these innovations. This brings me back to the mantra put forward by Professors Grosz and Simmons—to ensure that all affected stakeholders are present throughout the creation and implementation of the program. This means ensuring diverse perspectives in every stage of development, from conception to beta testing. But I think this work goes beyond making sure there are enough seats at the table. We need to actively support those individuals in their work so that they feel safe enough to bring their great ideas to the drawing board. Research has shown us how groups composed of individuals from diverse backgrounds create better products. Yet still, so many organizations stop short of providing the support these people need to do the great work they must do.

It's no surprise to anyone that careers in STEM are disproportionately filled with men of a certain background. As a woman and a leader in STEM, I have become accustomed to being the only woman in the room. This is due not just to my own curiosity about the field but to implicit biases that associate men with subjects like science, math, and engineering, and women with the arts and humanities. It's in school where these biases first become apparent, with only 20 percent of STEM majors in colleges identifying as women.[76] When these few women transition into the career field, they face larger hurdles that cause them to rethink their career choices when the leaders of the organizations are filled with skewed demographics. For example, over 70 percent of women in STEM have reported sexual

---

76　C. Hill, C. Corbett, and A. St. Rose, "Why So Few? Women in Science, Technology, Engineering, and Mathematics," American Association of University Women, February 2010.

harassment.[77] I think this would be cause for anyone to consider new opportunities. Yet, even in the most progressive organizations with strict ethics, women are often burdened with childcare responsibilities that keep them from being fully present while on the job.

It is difficult for a mother to devote all of her attention to one task as she juggles multiple roles: mother, employee, friend, and daughter. In itself, maintaining a career demands everything from someone, but a working mother must also raise children healthy in mind and body, not to mention getting their school supplies. A working mom can feel as though she is the only one weighted down on her legs with these sandbags at the starting line for a sprint. At NCSOFT, we opened our nursery school to reduce some of the burdens felt by our working parents, who are all encumbered in the same way. We did not create this nursery school to be a cure-all for an issue further complicated by the needs of each family and child. We sought to do our all in the hope that diversifying our efforts for the greater good might one day bring about a society where everyone feels supported.

This brings me full circle to the narrative of my vacant dormitory room at MIT. Over time, I managed to furnish it and establish camaraderie within my graduate cohort. The International Students Office (ISO) provided support but with inherent limitations, as it was designed predominantly from the perspectives of individuals already familiar with the American system. The discernible gap, however, highlighted the nuances that needed refinement in the pursuit of a more inclusive atmosphere.

When institutions create their diversity, equity, and inclusion (DEI) action, they often focus on the concept of "belonging." In belonging, we have the opportunity to make the greatest impact on the

---

77   RTI International. *Staying Power: Women in Science on What It Takes to Succeed,* December 2019.

STEM community by defining what community could mean to all of those who study, work, and do research. Together, we are all building this community, its rules, and the ways it functions in our world. As leaders in this field, we should work from the ground up to support individual academic endeavors as a whole no matter the student or employee's identity. DEI shouldn't just be about getting diversity in the door and leaving them to figure things out. We must ensure that the rules that govern how we operate in these spaces support every individual involved. And it starts with bringing together people who have been in different shoes and giving everyone a platform to be effectively involved. Gaming should not be an exception.

CHAPTER SEVEN

Cooperative Play

Online gaming brings us together where we play out our fantasies and desires, but it is also a system of support for those who need it.

Humans want to be together. It's in our nature to connect. Whether that be over shared ideas, interests, or communities, we have always found a way to each other. As children, our local playground was the place where we met up to play. With no limit but the amount of sunlight we had, we played with others similar in age. We'd learn about what our peers liked, and what they disliked. We invented games to explore parts of ourselves with each other. We sometimes even crossed boundaries and hurt our friend's feelings. When it was all over, we went home and started the whole day over again the next morning. This natural instinct to commune with each other through play has been with us throughout human history.

It's no wonder then that, with the advent of the internet, humans found a way to connect with each other in digital spaces. From the first internet forum to the emerging metaverse, we have always used the internet to connect with people from all over the world. As our spheres of interaction expand, we are introduced to new cultures, new ideas, and new perspectives that may challenge our preconceived notions. For some, this may be a welcome expansion for our minds, allowing us to see our "in real life," or IRL, communities with fresh eyes. For others, these new perspectives cause inner conflict, causing them to violently lash out at their computers without thought of the human they are harming on the other end. With this new human connection offered through our broadband connections, we must consider how we shape these spaces and how we can support each other—no matter what world we're in.

Our digital spaces offer us a cover. As mentioned in a previous chapter, spaces like MMORPGs and even Reddit forums offer users the opportunity to test out parts of their personalities. In these spaces, users can adopt new identities where they can act in ways that they'd never be able to in the real world. For some, this brings out bad behavior. Combine these negative intentions with the drive to compete that gaming inspires, and it's clear to see how unsportsmanlike behavior might occur. In fact, in 2020, 81 percent of gamers in the US admitted to witnessing some form of harassment from other players while engaging in online play—a sharp uptick from the 74 percent reported in 2019.[78] Just as on the playground, someone becomes the bully and someone becomes the victim. In our digital spaces, however, the bullies' identities are hidden, and the ramifications for harassment are not often as immediate as they are in the real world.

---

78   Anti-Defamation League (ADL). "Free to Play? Hate, Harassment, and Positive Social Experiences in Online Games 2020," November 2020.

In the same study, however, 95 percent of US gamers noted that they had positive experiences with others in the online world.[79] Indeed, friendships, partnerships, and even romantic relationships can be formed through online play. Within these games, players are also able to act out all the positive aspects of human relationships. In many of our offerings from NCSOFT, users have conducted in-game weddings between their avatars. Community celebrations throughout the year celebrate our diverse group of gamers and bring players together to get loot and rare equipment. Players collaborate with each other within their guild, an in-game team of players, to overcome tough bosses and raids. Through these activities, our gamers build communities of support that they might not have in the real world. In this way, play is no longer localized to just who is physically near you—it extends to the whole world.

> » **Friendships, partnerships, and even romantic relationships can be formed through online play.**

THE BARTZ LIBERATION WAR—A DIGITAL REVOLUTION

Online play, then, does not represent a good or a bad influence on human behavior, but instead, reveals something about the players. To illustrate this concept, let's look at the Bartz Liberation War, one of the biggest moments in the history of *Lineage II*, and the way it impacted the players that participated in the first revolution in MMORPG

79   Anti-Defamation League (ADL).

history. In 2003, we opened up *Lineage II* for beta access, based on the popularity of the original *Lineage* title, which was popular among Korean gamers. At the time, many *Lineage* users played in PC Bangs, LAN gaming centers where, for an hourly fee, one could play an online game. When we first opened up the Bartz server for *Lineage II*, legacy players from *Lineage* transitioned to the sequel to gather resources in the hunting fields and to level up a new avatar. One group of such players was the Dragon Knights (DK) clan, a fearsome guild of experienced players.

Within the first month of the opening of the Bartz server, the DK clan had reached the highest clan level and had become the most powerful guild on the Bartz server. Three months later, they teamed up with two other powerful clans to form DK United. Their aim was simple: to secure all in-game items and money for the clan and to keep other players on the server from leveling up. At the time, PC Bang players believed that power and domination were the keys to being successful at *Lineage II*. In that spirit, they dominated the hunting grounds, killing any non–DK United affiliated players that dared to level up their characters. They also slaughtered general players to suppress the strength of the players who were not in their guild. Through these tactics, DK United formed a dictatorship over the Bartz server that frustrated many players.

Before too long, news of the DK United tactics spread to players on other servers through message boards, blogs, and PC Bang chatter. At this time, Korean gamers saw online gameplay as a competition to be the strongest player on the server. In that sense, DK United was teaming up to ensure they were on top of the pack. Many *Lineage II* players, however, disagreed. They called out DK United tactics as unfair and just not fun. "Hunting fields are not DK's, but all players' possessions,'" wrote one commenter on a *Lineage II* freeboard.[80]

This and other comments began to rile up *Lineage II* players, who vastly outnumbered the high-level players of DK United. Over 86 percent of players on the Bartz server were below level forty. This was nothing compared to the average level of DK United clan members, which averaged around sixty-five. But with the tight hold that the clan had over resources needed to level up characters, there was little hope that this majority would be able to grow in power to overcome their rulers. Knowing that their strength was in their numbers, however, players from multiple servers began to plan a counteroffensive to the iron fist of DK United.

And thus, a resistance to the dictatorship was formed. A year after the formation of DK United's rule, hundreds of low-level players equipped with cloth armor and bone daggers began to swarm the holdings of the powerful clan. Dubbed Naebokdan, or the Long-Underwear Corps in English, these level-ten avatars overpowered the heavily armored members of DK United and began to take back their digital world. The Long-Underwear Corps's tactics were simple— overwhelm their high-powered foes with immense numbers. Even the most fearsome of their warriors were no match for wave after wave of hundreds of low-level characters sieging their castles.

Players from across servers came to the aid of the Bartz server, creating basic avatars with only the default armor that resembled thermal underwear, which is how the group came to be called the Long-Underwear Corps. With broken alliances, advanced battle tactics, and defecting members, the movements and behaviors of this online

---

80   Yoon Sang Cho, "Playing for Resistance in MMORPG: Oppositional Reading, Emergence, and Hegemony in the *Lineage II* "Bartz Liberation War" (thesis, Georgia State University, 2012).

resistance began to mirror real-world revolutions of years past. Some scholars have even compared the dress of these avatars to the "sans-culottes" of the French Revolution, when the lower classes dressed in trousers instead of silk pantaloons.[81] For almost four years, the Bartz Liberation War waged on, until, in March 2007, the final remnants of DK United were squashed in a battle at the Monastery of Silence.

In the Bartz Liberation War, players in PC Bangs across Korea shifted their online behavior from a self-focused plight to be the most powerful to a resistance based on ideals. Their resistance, spurred on by the involvement of the Long-Underwear Corps, was less concerned with traditional modes of clan warfare that were typical of *Lineage II* but was inspired by higher notions of equity and fair play. The Long-Underwear Corps had nothing to gain by their endless fight—no items, or new armor, or levels gained. Instead, they fought so that everyone could enjoy *Lineage II*. Their resistance had such an impact on the world of *Lineage II* that we decided to include it in the official lore of the game and several promotional materials. While this revolution had massive implications in the digital world of Aden, it also shaped the way that these players thought about real-world issues, as well.

While the online resistance of the Bartz Liberation War raged on, Koreans were taking to the streets to protest beef regulations in the free trade agreement between the United States and South Korea. Thousands of Koreans lit candles to call out what they saw as the Korean government's allegedly unethical policies on imported US beef products. The same forums that birthed the Long-Underwear Corps resistance were ablaze with talk about the candlelight protests. One comment from a user named Typhoon read, "I played in the Bartz server ... I am going to participate in the candlelight protest. There is also DK in [the] real world. I hope the Long-Underwear Corps people

---

81   Yoon Sang Cho, "Playing for Resistance."

are real." *Lineage II* players even took lessons from their online play to thwart the crowd control tactics of Korean police.

"We need to form a united and organized movement [like] In the Bartz Liberation War," mentioned a player in another forum post.[82]

Gamers who may not have been interested in social issues before the Bartz Liberation War were now passionate about fights for justice in the real world.

What can we learn about human behavior from this story? At its most basic level, the Bartz Liberation War contains elements of the clichéd story of good winning over evil. But it's also about how these players, immersed in *Lineage II*'s world of honor and pride, adopted these values into their gameplay, fighting for the underprivileged in both digital and real-world spaces.

Through play, gaming has the power to lift up a mirror, showing us who we really are, and who we can be. While gaming communities may have the capacity for harassment and abuse, the Long-Underwear Corps and their resistance prove that we need not be ruled by our most basic instincts. In fact, we can rise above our selfish impulses to help those in need. In the story of the Bartz Liberation Army, we see that people are eager to help out—whether that's online or IRL.

> » **Gaming has the power to lift up a mirror, showing us who we really are, and who we can be.**

---

82   Yoon Sang Cho, "Playing for Resistance."

ONLINE GAMING—A FORCE FOR GOOD

Online gaming can be and is a force for good in this world. As in the playgrounds of our childhoods, online gamers bond with each other over shared play and seek to support their colleagues. In these digital spaces, however, this support stretches across the world, increased tenfold through the power of a broadband connection. Online gaming communities raise funds for important charities and those in need. Guilds and clans support their struggling members not just in the game but also in real life. The communities built around these games have the power to inspire the best in us and cause change in the real world. Acknowledgment should be paid, then, to the positive impacts of online play.

One example of this force for good is Extra Life, a fundraising program of Children's Miracle Network (CMN) Hospitals. Their mission is to play games to change kids' health. At NCSOFT, we've worked with them countless times to raise funds for children in need. CMN comprises over 170 hospitals across the US and Canada. They help critically ill and injured children who are not covered by insurance get the care they need. Through their work in these hospitals, CMN arranges over thirty-two million treatments each year for children in dire health conditions. Every year, Extra Life Game Day serves as their premiere digital fundraising event, a twenty-four-hour charity stream to encourage players from various games to raise money for CMN.[83]

For Extra Life Game Day 2022, NCSOFT's Team ArenaNet engaged the *Guild Wars 2* community to raise more money than ever before for the important campaign. One of the first ways we engaged *Guild Wars 2* players was by providing in-game items for players who watched our Extra Life Twitch live stream. Hosted by our

---

83   J. Scharnagle, "*Guild Wars 2* Is Turning a Real-life 10-Year-Old Hero into an NPC for Charity," Dot eSports, October 2022.

Team ArenaNet developers, these live streams encouraged players to donate to CMN in exchange for in-game items, buffed stats for their characters, and other incentives. Our streamers even offered silly perks like shaving their heads or building a crown of spoons to inspire our gamers to give.

In addition to live streams, Team ArenaNet introduced April, a new NPC based on a CMN patient and *Guild Wars 2* player, to the world of *Guild Wars 2*. A ten-year-old survivor and champion over pneumonia, septic shock, and gangrene, this young warrior was brought to Team ArenaNet's attention through their partnership with CMN. After a brief conversation with April and her parents, the team got to work designing her NPC, upgrading her real-world prosthetic leg with in-game jade technology. Debuted in anticipation of Extra Life Game Day, her character was met with overwhelming support from the *Guild Wars 2* community. "Yay for positive wholesome things!" one player commented. "[Team ArenaNet] ... goes the extra mile for the community pretty often."

For over six years, Team ArenaNet has participated in Extra Life Gamer Day to raise money for these children in desperate need. Since then, they, along with the *Guild Wars 2* community, have raised over $500,000 for CMN. In 2022, they broke all their previous fundraising records. In just one day, they raised over $125,000 in direct donations to CMN, coming in second on the fundraising leaderboard of over 3,200 participating teams. It was also their most successful stream to date with 151,000 live views and over three thousand new Twitch followers. The goodwill of this community during this time shows me that gaming isn't just about the shiniest armor or the best weapon. It's about playing with people you enjoy and supporting the community that you inhabit online.

But it isn't just on Extra Life Game Day when the *Guild Wars 2* community gets involved. In fact, this MMORPG's community is known for seeking out ways to uplift their fellow players. There is a whole calendar of events throughout the year that gives these players a chance to connect over issues that bring them together. Team ArenaNet even designs "skins," aesthetic items that allow players to signal to others their support for each other. In-game Pride celebrations, for example, bring together LGBTQ+ players and guilds in common spaces in the digital world. For these celebrations, Team ArenaNet releases skins that feature the various flags of the LGBTQ+ community.

Another event like this was our partnership with the Seize the Awkward campaign for Mental Health Awareness Week. The campaign focused on building friendships among gamers and encouraging them to have conversations about mental health. The development team, however, wanted to extend the impact to the real world. The in-game event culminated as part of PAX East in Boston, where Team ArenaNet member and Twitch streamer Rubi Bayer participated in a panel discussion entitled "Build Your Guild: Make and Support Friends in Gaming."

Finally, the *Guild Wars 2* community is so engaged that they're helping and supporting each other even outside those weekly events. In 2017, a *Guild Wars 2* player came home from work to find a fire had caused extensive damage to her house. In a video the player posted on social media, she surveyed the destruction of her home to find that her collector's edition of *Nightfall*, an expansion for *Guild Wars 2*, was untouched. She also used the video on her Go Fund Me page to help her rebuild. Team ArenaNet caught wind of this player's misfortune, shared the post, and began crowdfunding themselves. Before too long, donations from the *Guild Wars 2* community came spilling in with one comment reading, "I found out about this via Twitter from Rubi

Bayer at ArenaNet. It's not much but I hope it helps, and I'll share it out. My wife and I's hearts go out to your family; we are deeply sorry for your loss."[84]

What these examples prove is that gamers are capable of more than just bullying and name-calling in the chat. These digital spaces that we inhabit, then, are not dissimilar to the world we experience every day. In fact, throughout this chapter, I have referenced things in a binary: digital spaces and real spaces. But the boundary between these two spaces may not be as defined as we think. We've seen the ways in which we play games together shapes gamer behavior in the Long-Underwear Troops and their resistance. In the *Guild Wars 2* community, we see an engaged group of players who uplift and support each other. Why then should all the focus be on the negative behavior of a loud group of players? Games reveal who we really are, but they also have the power to show who we want to be. We must allow the space for people to discover that on their own.

Since the advent of video games, politicians and policy makers have called for moderation of games, both online and offline. While we have robust codes of conduct for our multiplayer offerings at NCSOFT, we also understand that moderation is on a case-by-case basis. Human interaction is messy, and we're not always able to legislate or code away all our problems. Developers, users, policy makers, and anyone else involved must realize we all play a part in the way we use these tools like MMORPGs to connect with each other. As we build these digital worlds, we all have a responsibility to bring the best of ourselves to these communities. In doing so, we lay the groundwork for real-world connections that have roots in a virtual space.

---

84   Comment from MMO INKS on "Hunsucker House Fire Go Fund Me," December 2017, https://www.gofundme.com/f/hunsucker-house-fire.

CHAPTER EIGHT

Artificial Intelligence and Non-Playable Characters

In the mid-1960s, engineers at Massachusetts Institute of Technology's (MIT) Artificial Intelligence (AI) Lab had been working on a pet project of their colleague and mentor Richard Greenblatt, a master programmer and hacker who would later go on to work for the Defense Advanced Research Projects Agency (DARPA). Greenblatt, an avid chess player, wanted to test out whether a computer could be programmed to win a game of chess against a human. At the time, computer coding was brand new and this popular theory, first posited by Alan Turing, the grandfather of computer science, was a common project for many coders.

After many years of development, the MIT AI Lab students along with Greenblatt programmed MacHack IV in MIDAS, an archaic programming language based in a PDP-6 macro assembly. In the winter of 1967, the YMCA in Boston hosted the Boylston Chess Club Tournament, just over the river from the Cambridge home of the MIT AI Lab, and Greenblatt and his team had the perfect beta testing opportunity. They packed up the sixty-pound teletype Keyboard Send and Receive and headed off to register the machine as "Richard Q." in the weekend-long tournament. After four games, however, MacHack was bested three times (once by Chess Master Carl Wagner) and brought another game to a draw.[85] Later that month, the *Lewiston Daily Sun* ran a headline that read, "MIT Computer Loses to Human in Chess."

When MacHack IV played in the Boylston Chess Tournament, it was far from being the self-automated player we expect from our digital avatars today. Several engineers were needed to key in input and relay the program's output for the machine, which was remotely controlled by another team of engineers. The work of this team, and the supporting research of the AI Lab, laid the groundwork for the completely automated artificial intelligence we use and engage with today. While it might seem trivial, coding a computer to play a game became one of the foundational blocks of the study of AI. Just as play helps us learn as humans, so too has AI grown through its own style of play. And as AI has grown, we all have become more familiar with these automated playmates that help us grow and play.

The journey of AI in video games can be traced back to the rudimentary technologies that enabled player input and simulated non-playable characters (NPCs) within game environments. One of the earliest instances of AI in gaming was observed in the form of branching-tree decision-making. This allowed players to make choices that influenced the progression of the game's narrative, creating a

---

85   Rebecca Perry, "MacHack VI: Computer Chess and the Roots of AI," *Platypus Blog,* January 2020.

sense of agency and interactivity. Similarly, the introduction of NPCs, controlled by AI algorithms, added an element of unpredictability and challenge to games. These NPCs were often programmed with predefined behaviors and patterns, responding to player actions in predetermined ways.

As you probably already know, it's not just chess that computers play. Games from all genres have used foundational AI technology to challenge and intrigue players since that cold wintery night in Boston in 1967. As the arcade era dawned, games like *Galaga* showcased AI's potential to create dynamic and adaptable opponents. Alien ships, the enemies in *Galaga*, coordinated movements and formations based to evade the player. These movements, while only basic programming, exhibited a level of intelligence that kept players engaged. This kind of "automated computer player" became popular in arcade and console games like *Pac-Man*, *Mario Kart*, and others. While rudimentary, these opponents set the stage for more sophisticated AI implementations that had not yet been realized.

In massively multiplayer online role-playing games (MMORPGs) like *Lineage II*, NPCs are programmed to entice the player to delve deeper into the in-game world. By interacting with certain NPCs, the player is able to unlock undiscovered areas, attain new equipment, and take part in new clan battles. As mentioned in a previous chapter, these NPCs breathe life into the world of the game. They are carefully constructed characters based on deep algorithms that give the player the perception that the world of the game is vibrant and alive. They immerse the player in the digital world so that players can feel like their actions in the game have consequences. In a sense, these NPCs are citizens of a digital world where the player stands as a tourist.

In recent years, however, humans have been spending more and more time in these digital worlds—and not just to play. Music and entertainment sales largely happen online, while analog sales of compact discs are dwindling. And one day soon, digital banks will overtake brick-and-mortar banks. E-commerce, which was developed as a convenience, has become a staple in households across the world, generating over a trillion dollars of revenue.[86] While the COVID-19 shutdown forced many of us to move these chores into the digital space, the pandemic was only an accelerant. Technology was always going to create these digital spaces. With everyday interactions like banking, healthcare, and shopping moving away from the analog, humans are sharing more time in worlds populated by automated assistants that are not dissimilar to NPCs.

By playing and working with these machine learning programs, we all became more familiar with computers with agency and personality. Playing against the CPU character in *Mario Kart* made people more comfortable with automated assistants that live in their pocket or connected devices. Communicating with programs like Siri and Alexa became easier when we needed to set a timer or remind ourselves of something. Even Cortana, Microsoft's retired automated assistant, was born out of Microsoft's flagship game, *Halo*. In the game, Cortana served as the main player's guide through an alien galaxy, but in our world, she could not keep pace with her more popular competitors. Through these virtual assistants, however, our former playmates have become like an external brain helping us keep track of our days and giving us information about our real world.

And as we begin to complete more of our daily tasks online, digital assistants powered by machine learning abound. Traditional banking help desks are typically powered by basic chatbots that use branching-tree decision-making that resembles the arcade games of years past.

---

86   John Koetsier, "E-Commerce Retail Just Passed $1 Trillion for the First Time Ever," *Forbes*, January 2023.

But for many industries, that is also changing. With sophisticated conversational messaging technology, more organizations are looking to update their virtual assistants to better serve their customers. Companies like Amelia seek to evolve the automated service experience for enterprises in industries from healthcare to retail and everything in between.

The boundaries between the real world and our digital world are becoming more and more porous. Humans are becoming more comfortable buying, selling, and just generally existing in these digital worlds. In those digital ecosystems, there are already many forms of AI that we interact with, and more will be developed and deployed in the future. ChatGPT is only the beginning of what we can do with AI, and we must become more comfortable working in collaboration with our former playmates. Far from its early days playing chess in Boston, AI has become so prevalent that it is changing and molding the way we play video games today.

> » The boundaries between the real world
> and our digital world are becoming
> more and more porous.

NO MORE NPCs

With recent developments in AI and machine learning technology, AI's capability has extended far beyond the confines of NPCs and decision trees. Modern video games can use AI technology to create more realistic environments that adapt and change based on the player's input. Pushing this technology leads to more opportunities to understand how AI can be used and how it will affect our ever-growing digital world. There is so much that we still don't know about this new tool, and the more we play with it in our games, the more we can realize its potential.

Perhaps the most obvious way that AI is being used in gaming today is through NPC interaction and control. Ubisoft, for example, has already begun to investigate how they can use AI to generate real-time text responses from non-playable characters.[87] Yet, this only represents a small fraction of what AI can do with NPCs. With the way that AI is developing today, there may soon come a day where there are no more "non-playable" characters in an MMORPG. For example, an AI-controlled NPC could hold the key to an unexplored area of a certain game but will only reveal that after a specific interaction from a player. In this way, an AI player could learn how to play a game and develop their own strategies, objectives, and tactics that change in response to the player's actions.

Another way that AI can and is being used in games today is through dynamic environment development. Through AI algorithms, development teams can create landscapes and topography that react in real time to the player's input. This means that an AI can map out a whole continent of mountains, forests, rivers, and trees in a fraction of the time that a game designer can. But there's more—these same algorithms can also simulate weather patterns based on the player's location and action. Unreal Engine's MassEntity, which is available for beta testing, allows game developers to unlock these capabilities in their projects and much more. Another notable application is procedural content generation, where AI algorithms dynamically generate game environments, levels, and even narrative elements.

---

87   Aisha Malik, "Ubisoft's New AI Tool Automatically Generates Dialogue for Non-Playable Game Characters," Tech Crunch, March 2023.

This approach ensures that each playthrough feels fresh and unique, contributing to a sense of exploration and discovery.

Finally, AI and machine learning have become integral to the design of MMORPGs. These expansive digital realms rely on AI to manage vast amounts of data, coordinate interactions between players, and simulate ecosystems teeming with NPCs. This enables MMORPGs to provide a sense of realism and depth that would be very difficult without AI's computational power.

The proliferation of AI in video games is inextricably linked to the broader trend of digitization that has become more and more popular as new technologies become available. As our human lives become increasingly entwined with digital ecosystems, AI's presence continues to expand. Gamers who have interacted with AI-driven NPCs have developed a heightened familiarity with the technology, potentially making them more receptive to AI applications in other domains.

This growing familiarity with AI has paved the way for its increasing prevalence outside the realm of gaming. Organizations across various sectors are harnessing AI to manage massive datasets, extract insights, and optimize decision-making processes. In fields as diverse as healthcare, finance, and manufacturing, AI algorithms are revolutionizing operations and unlocking new possibilities. Consequently, the skills and comfort levels developed by gamers in interacting with AI could potentially translate into broader societal benefits.

While the potential of AI is undeniably promising, its widespread adoption also raises ethical concerns. The exponential growth of AI-driven technologies necessitates a proactive approach to ensure that the benefits are maximized while minimizing the risks. While the technology differs, we have already seen how fraudsters have taken advantage of users who may be unfamiliar with how virtual assistants operate, and their underlying technology. In 2020, Amazon brought a lawsuit against a ring of scammers who attempted to swindle Echo users out of $150 for protection insurance and set up fees that were not associated with the company.[88] Considering how frequently we interact with Alexa today and how AI is quickly replacing this technology, we must be vigilant to not fall into the same traps. If this is an example of the way we interact with these digital assistants, we can see how bad actors could exploit AI's capabilities for nefarious purposes. With its near unlimited potential, these scammers using AI could lead to privacy breaches, misinformation, and social manipulation.

To address these concerns, society must cultivate curiosity about AI rather than succumbing to anxiety. A well-informed and technologically literate populace can serve as a bulwark against the misuse of AI. Initiatives that promote AI education, critical thinking, and responsible AI development are essential to navigating the complexities of this evolving landscape.

> **» A well-informed and technologically literate populace can serve as a bulwark against the misuse of AI.**

AI's evolution through video games mirrors humanity's ongoing quest for innovation and progress. From humble beginnings as rudimentary decision trees and scripted NPCs, AI has matured into a dynamic force that shapes modern gaming experiences and extends its influence into various aspects of our lives. As the digital ecosystem expands and AI becomes increasingly pervasive, gamers' familiarity

---

88   Ben Fox Rubin, "Amazon Says a Group of Scammers Set Its Sights on Alexa Device Customers," CNET, May 2020.

with AI-driven NPCs positions them as early adopters and advocates for responsible AI integration.

The trajectory of AI in gaming exemplifies the potential for technology to enrich human experiences and capabilities. By embracing curiosity and cultivating a deeper understanding of AI, society can harness its transformative power while safeguarding against its potential pitfalls. As we venture into a future where AI-driven NPCs evolve and learn from player input, the lessons learned from gaming's AI evolution serve as a guiding light toward a world working in partnership with our most advanced technologies.

CHAPTER NINE

Gaming's Lens into the Future

In *Metal Gear Solid*, an action-adventure game published through Konami and developed by game director Hideo Kojima, the player takes on the role of a super soldier named Snake. In the game, Snake encounters terrorist groups, infiltrates their bases, and attempts to bring an end to their dangerous acts. To be successful, there are many occasions in which the player must evade detection from enemy forces. Stealth is imperative. There is, however, a piece of equipment that Snake encounters late in the game to aid in this. A stealth suit that renders him practically invisible helps the player remain undetected by hostile NPCs.

While this technology may seem out of science fiction, the fact is that the capability of such a suit exists today. Hyperstealth Biotechnology, a Canadian company that designs suits for militaries across the globe, has applied for a patent for a new "Quantum Stealth" material that refracts light waves, rendering whoever wears the material invisible. It is ultrathin, almost like a sheet of paper, and hides soldiers, tanks, and really anything from ultraviolet, infrared, and shortwave infrared waves. Described as a "broadband invisibility cloak," this material is easy and cheap to produce, making it desirable for every nation's military.[89]

This real-world stealth suit is an example of how nearly anything you can dream up can be made reality with enough time and effort. A concept that was once considered science fiction can now be used in real-world applications today. With the rise of AI, virtual reality, and other technologies, many innovations that were once thought to be "futuristic" are now becoming common. Video games allow us to play in these spaces of imagination where we can dream up new capabilities and push the limits of our human capability. Gaming gives us a lens into the future of what's possible and spurs on our spirit of innovation.

> **» Gaming gives us a lens into the future of what's possible**

Our growing digital world is another example of a past dream that has only now been realized. Across continents, we all go online to meet others, buy products, and do business. This bustling "digital commons," as we have seen before, has begun to encroach on our real world. Things we used to do in person have become more convenient to do online. As these two worlds continue to collide, gaming has shaped and molded what our online spaces look like, and how we interact in them. User experience, graphics, and frictionless technology have roots in the gaming space, but they have since grown

---

89   Kristin Houser, "Watch a Real-Life Invisibility Cloak Designed for Military Use," Futurism, https://futurism.com/the-byte/watch-invisibility-cloak-military-use.

beyond the industry. Good user experience, strong graphics, and an easy consumer experience are all common expectations when we go online. And with new innovations in gaming happening every day, the boundaries will continue to recede, creating new possibilities for our experience of humanhood.

As we discussed in previous chapters, user experience design, more commonly referred to as UX design, is a critical component of software development that focuses on creating intuitive, user-friendly interfaces. Gaming has played a significant role in shaping UX principles that have now become ubiquitous in popular programs and applications. One of the major ways that gaming UX has made its way into popular culture is gamification, in which game mechanics are used in nongaming contexts. Gamified applications engage users through reward systems and incentives that enhance their experience and keep their attention by injecting fun into their experience. As of today, gamification is table stakes for many organizations across industries. Many patient portals in healthcare industries have adopted gamification methods to encourage healthy behavior in their patients. Additionally, applications that gamify health tracking and encourage physical activity have empowered users to take charge of their well-being. For instance, wearable fitness trackers use gamelike incentives such as achievements and rewards to motivate users to achieve their health goals.

This gamification approach not only encourages healthy behaviors but also emphasizes the importance of user engagement and interaction. Lessons learned from gaming have led to the development of more interactive and engaging user interfaces in various software applications, enhancing user retention and overall satisfaction. This new style not only makes the mundane more fun; it also catches the eye of the user, just like a video game's advanced graphic style. In today's digital world, attention is currency, and the industry that learns how to keep eyes on their product comes out ahead. In that vein, the rapid advancement of graphics technology in gaming has continuously pushed the boundaries of visual spectacle and influenced various industries that require the attention of their customers.

In a previous chapter, I compared the size and scope of the video game industry to that of Hollywood's entertainment complex. While it seems that video game culture has become a source of inspiration for Hollywood, they're also using techniques and software first proven in the game design to give their movies and TV shows a visual pop. The Unreal Engine, originally created to make games, has found applications beyond interactive entertainment. Its advanced graphics rendering capabilities have been harnessed in the film industry to create stunning visual effects and immersive virtual environments. For example, *The Mandalorian*, one of Disney's premiere streaming programs, utilized the Unreal Engine to generate real-time digital backdrops, reducing the need for physical sets and enabling a seamless blend of live action and computer-generated imagery.[90]

This cross-pollination between gaming technology and filmmaking illustrates how gaming's pursuit of visual realism has paved the way for innovative approaches in industries beyond gaming. The demand for lifelike graphics in both gaming and movies has driven technological advancements in computer graphics and simulation, benefitting various sectors that rely on high-quality visual experiences. Gaming introduced to the general public the need for great graphics, and now that style of graphics is common. Video games' influence over the way we consume media in our digital age is broad and wide reaching. This

---

90   Jeff Farris, "Forging New Paths for Filmmakers on *The Mandalorian*, Unreal
      (blog), February 2020, https://www.unrealengine.com/en-US/blog/
      forging-new-paths-for-filmmakers-on-the-mandalorian.

influence, however, has also redefined the way we approach consumer experiences, particularly in the realm of e-commerce.

Nintendo, known for its innovative gaming consoles, introduced the concept of a frictionless shopping experience through its Nintendo Wallet system. This system allowed users to make purchases with a single click, streamlining the payment process and reducing barriers to completing transactions. This approach was later adopted and popularized by e-commerce giant Amazon, transforming the way we shop online. Nintendo Wallet's impact on online retail highlights gaming's role in shaping user behavior and expectations. By prioritizing convenience and minimizing steps in the purchasing process, gaming-inspired concepts have set new standards for seamless digital interactions in various industries.

Gaming and game design have consistently demonstrated their ability to predict innovations and influence various sectors, leaving a profound mark on user experience design, graphics technology, and consumer behavior. The integration of gaming principles such as gamification and intuitive interfaces has resulted in enhanced user engagement across applications. The pursuit of visual realism in gaming has driven advancements in graphics technology, impacting industries beyond entertainment. Furthermore, gaming's influence on frictionless shopping experiences has transformed the e-commerce landscape.

As technology continues to evolve, the lessons and insights gleaned from the world of gaming will likely continue to shape and inspire innovative solutions across diverse fields. The interconnectedness between gaming and innovation serves as a testament to the transformative power of interactive entertainment and design.

Finally, gaming has shaped the way we interact with each other both on and offline. MMORPGs bring together gamers from across the world and allow them to play in a big open space together.

People are able to find their tribes and play them, no matter where in the world they might be. Terms like *n00b* and *pwn'd*, which were commonly used in gaming chat, have gone on to affect the way we communicate with each other in the real world. In fact, gaming has made our worlds smaller, allowing us to have deeper connections with folks from around the world. With new innovations, however, we must ask ourselves—how will we change as we move in these new digital worlds?

THE WAYS WE MOVE IN THE DIGITAL WORLD

With all the advancements in computer technology, there are still some important things that keep us bound in the analog world. Keyboards, mice, game controllers, and other analog inputs are still necessary for us to move and play in these digital worlds. While gesture technology has been implemented in various controllers and game engines, we still require buttons to push to take finer action in the games we play. Even technology like the Oculus Rift, a virtual reality headset, has a set of controllers that allow the player to engage with the seamless world around them. Yet, the technology behind gesture control is becoming more advanced with every day and has the potential to change our world—and us—in ways we have yet to imagine.

Gesture technology, a recent advancement in human-computer interaction, has found substantial applications in the gaming industry, redefining gameplay experiences and user engagement. This technology utilizes natural human gestures to control and interact with digital interfaces, eliminating the need for traditional input devices like keyboards and controllers. Beyond gaming, gesture technology has extended to various industries, including the healthcare, education, and automotive industries. The evolution of gesture technology in gaming has broad-reaching impacts on user experiences and has transformative effects across diverse sectors.

Once something only thought of in *Star Trek*, gesture technology started with rudimentary motion-sensing controllers in gaming. At the 2009 E3 convention, a massive trade event for the video game industry, Microsoft announced their new motion-sensing device, the Kinect. Soon after that, Nintendo released the Wii and Wii U consoles, which relied heavily on the player's movement as input in gameplay. For players, this continued to break down the barrier between the world of the gamer and the world of the game. With current VR setups, gesture technology found a natural fit in VR gaming, enhancing presence and immersion. Gesture control introduced new dimensions to gaming, from physical fitness–based games to intricate hand-based spell casting in fantasy RPGs. This technology also democratized gaming, making it accessible to people with disabilities and diverse skill levels.

Immersing the user further and deeper into digital worlds is the consistent desire for game developers and gamers alike. And the rest of the world reaps these benefits as well. Gesture control bridges the gap between the real and virtual worlds, deepening player immersion and engagement. Physical gestures enable players to interact with games in ways that mimic real-world actions, enhancing realism and enjoyment. Multiplayer games leverage gesture technology for more natural social interactions, from virtual high-fives to nonverbal communication. Gesture-based gameplay challenges cognitive functions, promoting problem-solving, spatial awareness, and creativity. The emotional expressiveness of gestures enhances storytelling and character development, fostering a deeper connection between players and game worlds.

As gesture technology has matured in the gaming industry, it also has had impacts in areas like healthcare, education, and various other industries. In healthcare, surgeons use gesture-controlled simulations for skill development and training. Physical therapists also use gesture-based exercises to aid in rehabilitation.[91] For some stroke patients, virtual reality simulations allow them to practice repeated gestures in the hands and fingers, which are tracked by a motion-sensing algorithm to build their fine motor control after serious trauma. Finally, gesture-enabled devices facilitate telemedicine interactions and lead to clearer interactions between patient and healthcare provider.[92] This technology that tracks our movements has made it so that we are not only more immersed in an environment but that we better understand our own movements in the world.

In the world of education, gesture-based technology allows for new avenues for people who have diverse learning styles. While still in its nascency, educational gesture technology has the potential to transform classrooms into dynamic learning environments. Using gravity and infrared and motion sensors, an instructor may be able to reach a student whose learning style is more kinetic than the average individual's. Complex concepts can be simplified through interactive gestures, enhancing comprehension.[93] This style of gesture technology also breaks open new possibilities for job training in manufacturing industries where repeated actions are necessary. Gesture-guided

91   L. Sucar et al., "Gesture Therapy: A Vision-based System for Upper Extremity Stroke Rehabilitation," 2010, Annual International Conference of the IEEE Engineering in Medicine and Biology Society, doi: 10.1109/IEMBS.2010.5627458.

92   Karim R. Abdul et al., "Telepointer Technology in Telemedicine: A Review," *Biomedical Engineering Online*, March 9, 2013, doi: 10.1186/1475-925X-12-21.

93   N. S. Chen Kinshuk et al., "Evolution Is Not Enough: Revolutionizing Current Learning Environments to Smart Learning Environments," *International Journal of Artificial Intelligence in Education* 26 (2016): 561–581 (2016), https://doi.org/10.1007/s40593-016-0108-x.

assembly improves precision and reduces errors for folks on a manufacturing line. And for training and skill development, workers can learn complex tasks through interactive simulations.

Finally, gesture interfaces are also being implemented in automotive manufacturing to more streamline our commutes and make driving safer for everyone on the road. With the rise of infotainment systems in automobiles, more and more drivers are experiencing dangerous distractions that take their attention off the road. This distracted driving accounts for 25 percent of all driving accidents in the United States and almost four thousand fatalities each year.[94] Gesture and voice controls offer intuitive ways to manage in-car entertainment systems.

Gesture technology's journey from gaming innovation to multifaceted industry disruptor highlights its transformative potential. In gaming, gesture technology enhances immersion, engagement, and accessibility, setting new standards for user experiences. Beyond gaming, this technology offers intuitive and interactive interfaces for many industries. As gesture technology continues to evolve, its impact on human-computer interaction and the way we engage with technology redefines the boundaries of our possibility.

These gesture interfaces, rooted in game technology, connect us with the technology that we use every day. By bringing together our senses with the sensors and algorithms of our digital world, we are expanding our senses to match those of our digital counterparts. And it's not just gesture and touch that are being enhanced through these innovations. Even our hearing and sight are being augmented through new technologies that will change the way we perceive the world around us. With that in mind, we must ask ourselves: What does it

---

94   Pankaj Singh, "Automotive Gesture Recognition—The Next Level in Road Safety," ElectronicDesign, March 2019, accessed September 21, 2023, https://www. electronicdesign.com/markets/automotive/article/21807672/global-marketing-insights-automotive-gesture-recognitionthe-next-level-in-road-safety.

mean to be human in this new age, and what still can only humans do that computers cannot?

Which brings me back to the world of gaming. Video games provide humans with a sandbox for us to do the one thing that only humans can do: dream. Gaming pushes our imaginations, causing us to rethink the world that we live in. Through gaming, we reach into our deepest instinct to play that connects us, inspires us, and pushes us to dream up new possibilities. The creativity inherent in play has cultivated new technologies for thousands of years. It's this sense of wonder that will continue to fuel each new generation of innovations as we evolve with (and because of) new technology.

CONCLUSION

More Games, More Possibilities

As we have seen, games have changed humanity for the better. The Bartz Liberation War encapsulates the potent convergence of gaming and activism, underscoring how games galvanize collective action for meaningful change. *Hodoo English*, in turn, illuminates games' teaching potential while highlighting how they engender aptitudes and reshape cognitive paradigms.

Now that you have seen the power of play and gaming, how will you take these lessons with you into your daily life? No matter whether you're a veteran gamer or a newbie, there are countless benefits from installing some playfulness in your life. In this book, I've only outlined the ones that I have found, but what gaming benefits will you discover from your own experience? Video games fuel our sense of wonder, allowing us to dream big and create the next big thing.

» **Video games fuel our sense of wonder, allowing us to dream big and create the next big thing.**

As we end our time together, I am thinking back to the Royal Game of Ur, the ancient board game discovered centuries ago that I mentioned in the first chapter. The point of that game, which you can still find in toy stores now, was to race your opponent across the board, but that wasn't the only function of the game. These early game designers built a sense of wonder into their gameplay that feels powerful. Even in those early days, they saw the power of creativity that is inherent in play. And that is what I think separates a good game from a great game—the power to inspire wonder in its player.

Each day, new games are developed and marketed to fans across the world. As these games grow more sophisticated, the borders between the world of the game and our world grow porous, allowing things to slip between realities. We've seen how games in the past have spurred on innovations, which begs the question: What does a world inspired by our current games look like? Will it be artificial intelligences enriching our lives? Or new gesture technology that will seamlessly integrate us into the world? Or maybe something we haven't even discovered. To find out, the only thing we can do is play.